DEPARTMENT OF SOCIAL SECURITY

RESEARCH REPORT No. 62

UNEMPLOYMENT AND JOBSEEKING:

A National Survey in 1995

David Bottomley

Stephen McKay

Robert Walker

Social Security Unit
The Centre for Research in Social Policy
Loughborough University

London: The Stationery Office

First published 1997

ISBN 0 11 762452 7
ISSN 0961 5695

Views expressed in this report are not necessarily those of the Department or any other government department

Standing Order Service

Are you making full use of The Stationery Office's Standing Order service?

The Standing Order Service is a free monitoring of the publications of your choice from over 4,000 classifications in 30 major subject areas. We send you your books as they are published along with an invoice.

The benefits to you are:

- automatic supply of your choice of classification on publication

- no need for time consuming and costly research, telephone calls and scanning of daily publication lists

- saving on the need and the costs of placing individual orders.

We can supply a wide range of publications on standing order, from individual annual publications to all publications on a selected subject. If you do not already use this free service, or think you are not using it to its full capacity, why not contact us and discuss your requirements?

You can contact us at:

The Stationery Office
Standing Order Department
PO Box 276
London SW8 5DT

Tel 0171 873 8466; *fax* 0171 873 8222

We look forward to hearing from you.

CONTENTS

ACKNOWLEDGEMENTS

We would like to record our debt, on this project, to Andrew Shaw. He managed the project in its early days, developing the research instruments and steering the project into the field. He was ably assisted at Social and Community Planning Research by Jon Hales and latterly Andrea Nove. We would like to extend our thanks to them, and to their colleagues at Social and Community Planning Research. As ever, their interviewers delivered a high response rate to a long and difficult set of questionnaires. Contributions from the Institute for Employment Research and the Centre for Labour Market Studies are also acknowledged.

The survey has been managed by an inter-departmental Survey Management Group. We want to thank the past and current members of the steering group for their input, particularly Arthur Fleiss, Jenny Crook, Jenny Dibden and Gary Watson. We are also grateful to John Fletcher for his efforts in drawing the sample.

At the Centre for Research in Social Policy, Sharon Walker and Nigel Bilsbrough expertly managed the production of the report. Bruce Stafford read all our output, and provided insightful comments. Remaining errors and limitations are, of course, the responsibility of the three named authors.

Our greatest debt is to the almost 5,000 respondents who took part in the study. The study would have been impossible without their cooperation: we hope we have done justice to their views and experiences.

LIST OF ABBREVIATIONS USED IN TABLES AND FIGURES

BTEC	Business and Technology Education Council
BtWP	Back to Work Plan
CSE	Certificate of Secondary Education
ES	Employment Service
GCE	General Certificate of Education
GCSE	General Certificate of Secondary Education
GNVQ	General National Vocational Qualifications
GSVQ	General Scottish Vocational Qualifications
HNC	Higher National Certificate
HND	Higher National Diploma
IS	Income Support
LEC	Local Enterprise Council
LFS	Labour Force Survey
NI	National Insurance
NVQ	National Vocational Qualification
ONC	Ordinary National Certificate
OND	Ordinary National Diploma
RSA	Royal Society of Arts
SCOTVEC	Scottish Vocational Education Certificate
SIC	Standard Industrial Classification
SOC	Standard Occupational Classification
SVQ	Scottish Vocational Qualifications
TEC	Training & Enterprise Council
UB	Unemployment Benefit

SUMMARY

1 Introduction   Jobseeker's Allowance replaced Unemployment Benefit and Income Support for unemployed people on 7 October 1996. To enable the new system to be evaluated a national survey of unemployed claimants was conducted in Autumn 1995 which will be compared with a similar survey undertaken after Jobseeker's Allowance has been fully implemented. This report presents findings from this survey, providing a unique insight into the characteristics, attitudes and behaviour of unemployed claimants under the benefit regime which prevailed, with some modifications, from April 1988 to September 1996.

Jobseeker's Allowance   Jobseeker's Allowance aims to improve the working of the labour market, secure better value for money and enhance the service offered to unemployed people (Chapter 1.1). The new scheme has two components: Contribution-based Jobseeker's Allowance, a social insurance benefit that replaced Unemployment Benefit; and Income-based Jobseeker's Allowance which superseded Income Support for unemployed persons. The basic eligibility conditions are retained with others added. Claimants now have to sign a 'Jobseeker's Agreement' as a condition for receiving benefit. The rules relating to disqualification and disallowance have been strengthened and simplified. Finally, changed administration should ensure that claimants only need to visit one office in connection with their claim as an unemployed person.

The research   An extensive programme of monitoring, quantitative research and qualitative studies is being used to evaluate Jobseeker's Allowance. The main quantitative component comprises a 'before and after' design in which the experiences of two separate but nationally representative samples of unemployed people are compared under the old and new benefit regimes (Chapter 1.2). The unemployed are defined as the 'claimant unemployed', that is persons receiving Unemployment Benefit and/or Income Support because they are unemployed, or who are receiving National Insurance Contributions credits on account of unemployment, under the pre-Jobseeker's Allowance system.

Respondents in each sample are to be interviewed twice with an interval of six months. This report relates only to the analysis of the first (wave) interview with the first sample (cohort), comprising 4,876 respondents and 1,495 partners. A response rate of 75 per cent was achieved for claimants and the figures presented are weighted to provide the best attainable national estimates (Appendix A).

Although providing only a first step in the evaluation of Jobseeker's Allowance, the results presented in this report are important for two reasons (Chapter 1.3). First, they relate to what is probably the largest and most detailed survey of the experiences of unemployed claimants and their families ever conducted in Britain. Second, they offer numerous pointers to the potential of Jobseeker's Allowance to stimulate real change in the attitudes and behaviour of unemployed claimants.

2 The characteristics of unemployed claimants

For technical reasons (see Appendix A) two separate samples were drawn which throughout most of the report are merged to provide a cross-section of the unemployed. The 'flow' sample comprised respondents who had claimed benefit no more than two weeks before the sample was drawn. These respondents are termed 'new claimants' and occasionally reference is made to the circumstances and characteristics of this group. The second sample was drawn from the stock of unemployed claimants. However, the two samples were merged and appropriately weighted to provide estimates for the 'stock' of claimants, a cross-section through the entire unemployed population (Chapter 2.1).

Social and demographic characteristics of unemployed claimants

The characteristics of the flow and stock are compared and contrasted in Chapter 2. For the most part, the profile of the two groups is very similar but the differences are telling. Whenever respondents with particular characteristics are disproportionately represented among the stock, as compared with the flow, it suggests that, on average, they have longer spells of unemployment. Men, for example, comprised 74 per cent of the stock but only 66 per cent of the flow. On average the stock was also slightly older and included greater numbers of people living alone (24 per cent compared to 16 per cent). There were no differences by ethnic origin.

Only 25 per cent of the stock of unemployed claimants had dependent children. Sixty-one per cent of respondents in the stock had no partner and single people living with their parents were the largest group of all, comprising 27 per cent of the stock and 34 per cent of the flow. However, since the sample was drawn in the late summer (of 1995), this may be partly picking up a significant number of ex-students, who would tend to have short spells on benefit.

Eight per cent of the stock had never worked. Of those who had, former manual workers outnumbered non-manual workers by 1.6:1. Only two per cent of claimants had held professional positions but 21 per cent had worked in managerial or technical jobs. Respondents from non-manual occupations were under-represented in the stock, indicating shorter spells on benefit. Thirty-one per cent of the stock had no qualifications at all but the proportion of new claimants with at least basic qualifications (77 per cent) appears to have increased compared with earlier cohort studies of the unemployed, though this could be reflecting a sizeable inflow of ex-students at the time the sample was selected.

At the time of interview, 28 per cent of the claimant stock had been unemployed for less than three months and 60 per cent for a year or less (Chapter 2.3). Forty per cent had had a previous spell on unemployment-related benefit. New claimants included a disproportionate number (54 per cent) who had been unemployed before: evidence that a significant group repeatedly move in and out of work. Indeed, on average, new claimants had been on benefit for over seven months in the two years before their current claim.

Of course, claimants who were still unemployed when interviewed will have spent even longer on benefit by the time they eventually leave. Examining previous spells of unemployment experienced by new claimants in the two years before interview offers some insight into the true length of completed spells. For flow respondents (those recently unemployed), the median length of previous completed spells was nine weeks compared with 26 weeks for the stock of claimants (those currently unemployed).

At the time of interview 76 per cent of claimants received Income Support including seven per cent who also received Unemployment Benefit. Twenty-six per cent of new claimants received Unemployment Benefit alone. Six per cent of the stock were claiming National Insurance credits only (Chapter 2.3.3).

After at most two to three months had elapsed between sample selection and interview, 36 per cent of 'new claimants' had ceased claiming benefit: 22 per cent had found full-time employment, eight per cent part-time work (which included one per cent mixed with education) and three per cent education (Chapter 2.4). Whilst only eight per cent of the flow had moved into part-time work, this represents one-quarter of the outflow from benefit, and a higher proportion of those moving into work. However, only 20 per cent of the stock of claimants had moved off benefit by the time of interview. Half this number had moved into full-time employment, with three per cent having moved into part-time work. Part-time work therefore represented about one-sixth of the outflow from the stock, and one-quarter of those moving into paid work.

Fifty-seven per cent of the stock of claimants had had paid work at some point in the two years before interview, and 48 per cent had had a full-time job during this period. Fourteen per cent had engaged in full-time education and seven per cent had spent time out of the labour market on health grounds: four per cent to take on caring responsibilities and nine per cent for other reasons. More of the new claimants (79 per cent) had worked over the same period. There was a close correspondence between what respondents considered to be their 'usual job' and the one they were doing immediately before becoming unemployed which means that there was little evidence, at least to date, of progressive downgrading or de-skilling.

Where possible the partners of claimants were interviewed (Chapter 2.5). In households where neither partner was employed, it was typical for only one partner to be seeking work. In the flow sample 75 per cent of partners were female compared with 85 per cent of those in the stock.

There may be important interactions between the employment status of men and women in couples, and a separate Institute for Employment Research project is investigating such links. By the time of interview *both* parties were in work in 27 per cent of the households in the flow sample and in 11 per cent of those from the stock: typically this meant the unemployed claimant returning to work, with a partner already in work. At the same point, 23 per cent of flow households and 19 per cent of the stock had one partner in work, education or training and the other unemployed and looking for work.

3 Labour market background

Employment histories are hard to characterise but are important for understanding the routes by which people become unemployed. Asked to choose a statement that described their experience, the largest number (including the majority of older respondents) said they had mostly had 'steady jobs' (Chapter 3.1). While seven per cent of the stock said that they had never before been unemployed, 16 per cent, more often the young, reported that they had 'spent more time unemployed than in work'. More than one in ten (13 per cent), and more of the long-term unemployed said that they had been repeatedly 'in and out of work'.

Turning to the route taken on to unemployment, 60 per cent moved directly from employment, ten per cent from a training programme, eight per cent from education and 23 per cent from activities outside the labour market (Chapter 3.2). Twenty-three per cent of those who claimed benefit after a spell of employment had been made redundant and nine per cent had lost their jobs because their company stopped trading (Chapter 3.4). Twenty-seven per cent came to the end of a temporary job or fixed period contract and 16 per cent resigned.

Respondents becoming unemployed straight from education naturally tended to be younger but also included more women and members of minority ethnic groups (Chapter 3.2). Of this group 29 per cent had been studying for a degree and ten per cent for a Higher National Certificate or Diploma, while five per cent had been doing 'A' levels – although the August sampling date may be inflating these figures.

Reflecting the propensity of unemployment to affect some industries and occupations more than others, the jobs from which respondents came were not representative of those in the whole economy (Chapter 3.3). Professional and managerial groups were comparatively rarely unemployed (although they still accounted for 17 per cent of claimants) whereas plant and machine operators were disproportionately numerous. The composition of the claimant stock, and to a lesser extent the flow, also reflected the continuing recession in the construction industry, and the temporary nature of much construction work. Only 22 per cent of claimants had had managerial or supervisory duties.

The average weekly earnings of respondents prior to unemployment had been £172 for male claimants and, reflecting in part shorter hours worked, £118 for women. Former earnings peaked between the ages of 45 and 55, earlier for women. The reported incomes of people who had been self-employed were noticeably higher (£200–£249 per week) although a different type of measure was used.

4 Rules, responsibilities and obligations

Jobseeker's Allowance makes more explicit the job-seeking conditions in unemployment benefits. It also removes automatic access to hardship payments in cases that are sanctioned, potentially increasing the effect of such action. Respondents were asked about their understanding of rules under the system of Unemployment Benefit and Income Support, and their experience of the system of penalties under the same system.

Understanding the rules

Open questions were asked about the rules relating to 'signing on', 'actively seeking work' and 'availability for work' (Chapter 4.1). Few responses were focused specifically on the rules governing signing on. Only three 'rules' were mentioned by more than a sixth of respondents: the requirements to sign off when employed (30 per cent); actively to seek work (30 per cent); and to declare work undertaken on benefit (18 per cent). Thirteen per cent could not remember any rules. The rules with most salience related to the requirement to report changes affecting eligibility for benefit, notably finding a job, but few people mentioned any aspect of the conditionality of benefit. People with educational qualifications were more likely to recall some rules.

Reflecting on the requirement actively to seek work, most respondents did no more than substitute simpler words, 52 per cent said 'looking for vacancies' and 27 per cent 'to look for work'. However, a substantial minority noted that the term 'actively' applied to their behaviour when they talked of the need to 'make an effort' to find work. Generally respondents differed little in the meanings they attached to actively seeking work. Respondents thought it right that claiming benefits was dependent on taking active steps to find work, but felt themselves to be sufficiently self-motivated to do this, rather than needing to be cajoled by the threat of sanctions.

Forty-eight per cent of respondents recognised the need to be able to start work immediately though only 21 per cent spontaneously recalled that under some circumstances they had to accept any job. Awareness of the former condition was greatest among those who had been on benefit for between one and two years.

It is possible that more in-depth questioning might have revealed that respondents had a greater understanding of the conditionality of benefit than the survey suggests. However, it is apparent that the requirement to seek and to be ready to take up employment as a condition of benefit is certainly not in the front of people's minds. Nevertheless, 94 per cent recognised that it was claimants' 'responsibility to look for a job'.

Disallowance and disqualification   People may be disallowed benefit for failing to meet the labour market conditions or disqualified if, through doing or failing to do something, they become or remain unemployed (Chapter 4.2). We have already seen that respondents, whilst sensing the broad details of the rules, were generally unfamiliar with the details. Eighty-four per cent of respondents were at least vaguely aware of the fact that their benefit could be affected by certain types of behaviour, but with little further knowledge: 43 per cent apparently did not realise that benefit could be reduced (as well as be stopped altogether).

There were also different responses, depending on whether respondents were asked an open question about rules, to investigate their spontaneous knowledge, or whether they were asked questions specifically about sanctions. Respondents did not always appear to link the overall rules with reasons for sanctions. The latter approach tends to give higher figures. When asked about sanctions, 35 per cent of claimants knew that benefit could be stopped for not actively seeking work but no other labour market consideration was mentioned in more than an eighth of the interviews; 12 per cent of respondents noted sanctions for refusing a training course, 11 per cent for not signing on, seven per cent for refusing a job offer and six per cent for not being available for work.

There were small variations in the beliefs of claimants receiving Income Support and those getting only Unemployment Benefit, and between respondents who had been claiming benefit for different periods. Almost certainly many people did not properly distinguish between eligibility for benefit and sanctions for non-compliance, abuse or fraud (for example, not declaring earnings).

A quarter of respondents reported that they had initially had their benefit stopped or reduced but only between 30 per cent and 40 per cent of these, that is perhaps eight per cent of the entire sample, appear likely to have been disqualified or disallowed on labour market criteria (Chapter 4.3). The most important reason, given by 22 per cent of all those who received no or reduced benefit, was voluntarily leaving a job. Many of those affected (61 per cent) by disallowance or disqualification had not suspected that they would be; typically, of course, the sanction would have resulted from actions taken before they had any contact with the Jobcentre (such as leaving a job voluntarily), particularly those who had not been unemployed before. Moreover, understanding of a wide range of rules has been found to be limited. The proportion surprised by the penalty was highest among those who had been disallowed on the grounds of not being available for work (72 per cent) and those who had been dismissed (63 per cent) and lowest among those who had resigned voluntarily (48 per cent). The people affected by 'sanctions' were more likely to be young, single or poorly skilled than the sample as a whole.

The lack of knowledge of the principles underlying benefit receipt does not necessarily mean that claimants would reject them; indeed the survey suggests strong support for the principle of conditionality, though less commitment to the idea that claimants should be denied benefit after resigning from a job (Chapter 4.4).

5 Dealings with the Employment Service and the Benefits Agency

Jobseeker's Allowance is intended to harmonise the systems used by the Benefits Agency and Employment Service. It develops aspects of the previous administration such as 'active signing' and interviews with Client Advisers. The Jobseeker's Agreement becomes a condition of benefit receipt, unlike the Back to Work Plan under the system of Unemployment Benefit and Income Support. So, how well did those procedures work?

Making a claim

Seventy per cent of respondents made one or two visits to receive benefit (or National Insurance credits only) and five per cent made five or more (Chapter 5.1). However, only 18 per cent of people were required to visit more than one office. The number who felt that they had had to spend a lot of time going between offices fell from 44 per cent of those who applied for benefit before 1990, to 18 per cent of those who made their claim in the third quarter of 1995.

Respondents who made more than two trips included disproportionate numbers of first time claimants, people without telephones, older persons and those who reported themselves to have been in and out of work. Respondents who received Income Support and Unemployment Benefit were also over represented among those making more visits but the number simultaneously receiving both benefits was small (four per cent of recent applicants).

New claims interviews

A key stage in the application process is the interview with a New Claims Adviser. Three-quarters of respondents applying for benefit in late Summer 1995 could remember their interview. Recollection of the interview was higher among those who had not been unemployed before, and lower among younger claimants. Forty-six per cent of those remembering the interview thought that the main purpose had been to check their eligibility and 15 per cent to check the claim form. Fourteen per cent said the main purpose was to get help to find a job and seven per cent believed that it was to 'make' claimants look for work.

Seventy per cent of recent applicants recalled the Back to Work Plan and two-thirds of respondents remembered being told about the rules relating to actively seeking work and availability for work. Only a minority said that they had been advised about effective job-search (38 per cent) or in-work benefits (17 per cent).

Twenty-three per cent of respondents felt that the interview had helped them decide on the sort of work to look for, but it was these who were most likely to recall the more pro-active elements of their interview. A large proportion of recent applicants (82 per cent) were confident that they knew what was expected of them in relation to job-search. Thirty-three per cent of people claimed to take action as a direct result of the interview, 35 took no action at all and 32 per cent did what they would have done anyway. The most negative response came from people with a long history of unemployment, those without a previous job and former managers. Respondents taking positive action included people who could recall being given advice by their New Claims Adviser. It will be interesting to see how far these actions affected whether people left unemployment: an issue we will return to with the second wave of data.

Back to Work Plans Eighty-eight per cent of claimants who could remember agreeing a Back to Work Plan had used it, including 57 per cent who said that they had followed it unreservedly. Those who did not follow it, on the other hand, were most often those who had the most tenuous experience of the labour market. However, only 41 per cent of those who adopted their Back to Work Plan found it useful. Of those who did not, 38 per cent considered it to be of no practical value, 31 per cent considered that the plan was common sense and 17 per cent said that they would have done the same things in any case.

Respondents differed little in their reactions to the Back to Work Plan. There was one exception. The proportion who considered it to be common sense declined with the length of time out of work, while the proportion who thought it to be of no practical value increased.

Signing on Ninety-four per cent were required to sign on in person each fortnight (Chapter 5.2). However, as already noted in response to an open-ended question, few people had previously given much thought as to why this should be so. When asked in a closed question about the purpose of signing on, no single response was given by as many as half of the sample: 46 per cent and 34 per cent respectively believed that it was to check that they were still available for work and seeking it, and 25 per cent saw it as a way of finding out whether claimants were illicitly working. Only ten per cent mentioned the possibility of being told about vacancies and seven per cent being given advice.

Respondents were asked about the last time that they signed on and specifically about four elements contained in the 'active signing' protocol. Only 42 per cent could remember any of the topics being covered, a proportion which ranged from 17 per cent to 96 per cent according to the office where they had signed on and also seemed to vary according to claimants' previous work history. Thirty-five per cent of respondents remembered being asked about their job-search and 13 per cent about action that had previously been suggested. Fourteen per cent were given advice or information and eight per cent were told about specific vacancies. If these replies are taken to reflect what actually happened, it would appear that staff were focusing their attention on moderately skilled manual workers, and perhaps those with a history of sickness and injury, but not linking their approach to the length of time that a person had been unemployed.

Respondents who had already moved off benefit were more likely than others to report that they had received pro-active intervention at their last signing on; the differences were small but statistically significant. In fact, 40 per cent who recalled pro-active elements said that the discussion had affected their behaviour. Of these, 36 per cent had applied for a job, 11 per cent for a training course and five per cent had taken up a place on Training for Work or Community Action. In addition, 17 per cent had looked at job displays in the Jobcentre and 15 per cent had sought work in other ways.

Restart interviews People on benefit for six months are invited for an interview with a Client Adviser. Seventy-seven per cent of respondents who had been out of work for between six and 12 months had had one (Chapter 5.3). That said, 18 per cent of those unemployed for a year or more could not recall ever having an interview. Forty-eight per cent of those who had attended an interview with a Client Adviser considered their last one to have been helpful or very helpful. Those who were most appreciative included respondents aged over 55 and those who had never before been unemployed. The most critical were former professional people and managers and those who had been in and out of work, or mostly held casual jobs.

Forty-three per cent of respondents said they took action as a result of their last interview with a Client Adviser, 42 per cent did nothing, while 15 per cent did what they said that they would have done anyway. Responses to the interview did not seem to differ systematically with the characteristics of claimants. Of those who responded positively, 35 per cent applied for a job, 22 per cent joined a Jobclub and 20 per cent looked for work in various ways.

Client Advisers can both offer advice and direct claimants to take particular actions although it is not clear that respondents clearly distinguished these two activities. However, it would appear that a third of respondents who had been unemployed for over three months had been advised to attend a government or TEC programme, a proportion that rose to 57 per cent among respondents with a self-professed history of sickness.

Thirty-five per cent of respondents believed that they had been *directed* to take a particular course of action, a proportion that changed with the length of time people had been claiming benefit with a marked increase after 12 months. In 50 per cent of cases the directive was to join a Job Club, with 14 per cent being told to apply for training and another seven per cent to go on a Training for Work or Community Action scheme. People directed to training courses included comparatively large numbers of former manual workers, people without any formal qualifications and respondents with a history of health problems. Skilled non-manual workers, and hence women, were under-represented.

Six per cent of respondents said that on some occasion they had been directed 'to apply for a certain job', although this turns out to include respondents who were asked to expand the range of jobs they applied for, or to join a Job Club. The group as a whole included relatively large numbers of people who had not previously worked, claimants without qualifications and those who had done semi-skilled or unskilled work.

6 Looking for work

A key objective of Jobseeker's Allowance is to improve the ways in which unemployed claimants look for work and the research provides baselines against which future behaviour might be assessed.

Attachment to work At the time of interview 80 per cent of respondents in the sample were still claiming benefit and 93 per cent of these said that they were looking for work (Chapter 6.1). Two per cent had stopped because they had found a job but not yet started, two per cent because they did not want to work and three per cent were not looking for no apparent reason.

The main reasons why people did not want to work were ill-health (24 per cent), caring responsibilities (13 per cent) and study, reasons that, a priori, might suggest that they were not in fact available for work. Thirteen per cent gave no reason and might similarly not be genuinely available. Only the fact that they did not want to work distinguished this group of respondents from those who did want employment.

Thirty-two per cent of claimants who said that they were not looking for work even though they wanted a job had nevertheless sought work within the last four weeks, suggesting that their inactivity was temporary. Thirty-eight per cent gave temporary or long-term illness (15 per cent) as the reason for not seeking work, 19 per cent the training course that they were attending and 15 per cent study. Nine per cent mentioned the lack of jobs and seven per cent a lack of suitable jobs, while five per cent felt that they would be financially worse off if they got a job. One per cent were concerned about the effect of getting a job on their partners' benefits.

Activities to find work Eighty-nine per cent of people seeking work had looked in the local press the week before interview, 71 per cent had visited the Jobcentre (rather more than the 50 per cent who would have needed to visit in order to sign on) and 44 per cent had consulted the jobs pages of the national press (Chapter 6.2). Around a third had contacted employers and tapped into informal networks. Only 52 per cent kept a record of their job-search, something strongly encouraged under Jobseeker's Allowance.

But there were limits on what people could do, with 39 per cent mentioning financial constraints, including 34 per cent who specifically noted travel costs and fares, and six per cent telephone costs. Six per cent complained of lack of transport, three per cent about where they lived, and five per cent about an absence of suitable vacancies.

Four per cent of respondents included health as a constraint on job-search. However, when asked directly, 25 per cent said that they had a health problem or disability that affected the type of work that they could do; higher than in previous research such as the Employment Service National Customer Satisfaction Survey (Nove with McKay, 1995). The large majority of this latter group (84 per cent) thought that the condition would persist for at least a year.

Sixty per cent of partners, more of those not in work, considered that they helped their partners seek work. Most of the help described was of a practical nature – 49 per cent mentioned looking for vacancies in newspapers and 11 per cent assistance with application forms – perhaps because emotional support was taken for granted. Only two per cent admitted to pressurising their partners to look for work.

As regards overall strategy 75 per cent of applicants felt that it was better to concentrate on 'working hard on a few applications' rather than to submit large numbers 'in a hurry' and appeared to follow this strategy (Chapter 6.3). Those unemployed for less than six months were more likely to say this than those unemployed for longer, but the differences were quite small. As the length of time on benefit increased, so respondents came to emphasise the importance of luck over effort in determining the likelihood of getting a job and as many as 53 per cent confessed that they 'sometimes stopped making applications for a while'. On the other hand, there was no evidence that long-term recipients spent less time looking for work or submitted fewer applications. On average, people devoted six and a half hours each week to seeking work and writing applications and typically they had submitted three applications in the four weeks prior to interview. Five per cent, however, had made over 30 applications while four per cent had made none.

Forty per cent of people who had applied for at least one job in the month before the survey managed to obtain an interview during this period, although 88 per cent of people were unsuccessful in getting an interview. The clear majority (84 per cent) of respondents had not received any job offers during the four weeks before the survey.

The perspective offered by the second wave survey should make it possible better to assess the kinds of claimant who are most successful in their job-search. Already comparisons between new claimants and the stock has generated several hypotheses (Chapter 2.2). These received confirmation from an analysis of the ratio of interviews to applications and the ratio of job offers to interviews. New claimants and women featured in the successful group for both interviews and job offers, while skilled non-manual workers were more likely than most to obtain an interview and those with qualifications or who had previously worked in management, in the technical professions or in the army were most frequently offered a position following interview.

Flexibility Large majorities of respondents seeking employment were looking exclusively for full-time jobs (68 per cent) and to work as employees (78 per cent) (Chapter 6.4). Twenty-one per cent were prepared to pursue self-employment including three per cent for whom it was a preference. Twenty-seven per cent were looking for either full-time or part-time work and five per cent, two-thirds of them women, specifically wanted a part-time job. On the other hand, a third of respondents were willing to work more than 40 hours. Seventy-one per cent would have accepted a temporary post.

Respondents generally seemed flexible about working conditions; around 80 per cent were willing to consider working shifts and weekends and 68 per cent night work. However, people were less prepared to work away from home or to move; only 35 per cent were prepared for the latter option while another 17 per cent were willing to consider it. Moreover, partners were generally less flexible than claimants about the kind of work that their partners should accept, especially where this might impact on home life: only 28 per cent of partners would countenance working away from home, compared with 54 per cent of claimants.

Claimants' flexibility was not clearly related to the length of time they had spent on benefit. While longer term claimants may have been more willing to depart from their usual occupation they seemed to be more stringent as to the working conditions that they were prepared to accept. Respondents living in areas with the very highest levels of unemployment were the most flexible about working conditions.

Respondents were asked for the wage that they were expecting to get on their return to work (the median was £140) and the lowest that they would be prepared to accept (a median of £120). Responses were clearly influenced by past incomes: professional people for example were expecting a wage of £202 per week and would not accept less than £179 whereas claimants who had previously worked in unskilled manual jobs wanted £140 but would have accepted £112. A regression analysis, conducted separately for respondents who had previously worked and those who had not, revealed that the minimum wage that people said that they were prepared to accept also depended on claimants' ages and domestic circumstances, and in the latter group, on their qualifications and the local unemployment rate.

Finally, respondents were asked about any concerns that they might have about moving off benefit into work. The more common responses had to do with money, notably work expenses, Council Tax payments and the need to bridge the time until the first pay day. Others had to do with the uncertain prospects of work and fear that they might be forced once again to claim unemployment-related benefits.

Prospects of obtaining work
On the whole, respondents were fairly negative about their chances of a speedy return to work (Chapter 6.5). Thirty-eight per cent thought that their prospects were either 'good' or 'very good', yet 56 per cent felt they were either 'bad' or 'very bad'. Men, perhaps justifiably in the light of the evidence already presented, were more likely than women to take an extremely negative view of their future. Likewise, older claimants may have been realistic in viewing their prospects more unfavourably than the young; more than half of those aged 55 describing their chances of returning to work as 'very bad'.

Some differences were also found between regions of the country with a higher proportion of respondents from London and the South-East and the Eastern region taking a positive view of their own prospects. These regions stand in marked contrast to the North-East, the South-West and Wales. Negative views prevailed in the areas of highest unemployment.

Respondents' assessment of their own chances of returning to work were compared with those of all claimants in the same area. There was much agreement, for only a quarter rated their own prospects more favourably than their neighbours' and just five per cent thought their chances to be worse. However, the length of time that a person had already been out of work may have some small effect on attitudes: the longer a person had been unemployed the less hopeful they were about their chances of returning to work. Women tended to express more polarised views than men, but older claimants were generally less optimistic. Partners of main respondents largely agreed with the assessments of their partners' prospects.

7 Activities while signing on
It may be advantageous for some unemployed claimants to undertake part-time work, study or voluntary work while claiming. This may improve their chances of finding full-time work, an issue this evaluation will need to address with longitudinal information. Chapter 7 analyses participation in each of these activities. At the same time the government is determined to prevent people from illicitly working while claiming benefit, or abusing the system in other ways.

Employment
In all, 13 per cent of respondents said they had done some work, legitimately or otherwise, at some point while claiming (Chapter 7.1). However, 36 per

cent of those who had not worked did not realise that it was possible to do so. At the time of interview four per cent of respondents were working while claiming benefit; the largest number (28 per cent) worked ten to 12 hours and 79 per cent were employed for less than 16 hours. Child-care, cleaning and operating check-outs were common occupations.

It would appear that at least nine per cent of those who were working and claiming while receiving benefit were employed for more than the hours permitted (earnings ranged from £10 to £80) while another 14 per cent did not report the extent of their working. Too few respondents were working illicitly to be able to report on their characteristics. However, women (17 per cent) were more likely to work than men (12 per cent), perhaps because of the kind of jobs available, as were those with background as self-employed (21 per cent) or as a casual worker (19 per cent). Those who worked tended also to be older than the norm.

Voluntary work Eight per cent of respondents were engaged in voluntary work at the time of interview or immediately before they found employment (Chapter 7.2). Seventy-seven per cent worked unpaid for between one and 12 hours each week (the median was six hours), although 18 per cent were engaged in volunteering for over 16 hours. Those respondents involved in voluntary work were, as other studies have shown, more likely to be female rather than male, older rather than younger, and with academic qualifications and a history of professional, managerial or technical employment.

Although, overall, only 38 per cent of respondents felt that voluntary work increased the chances of obtaining full-time employment, significantly more (54 per cent) of those who had done voluntary work believed that it did. Young people were less often engaged in voluntary work but they were more likely to think that voluntary work would help them secure paid employment.

Taking part in education Fourteen per cent of respondents were undertaking some study whilst unemployed (Chapter 7.3) or just prior to signing off. This comprised 15 per cent who were studying and signing on, and ten per cent who were studying just before they signed off.

The median time they were spending on a course (that is excluding personal study), or were spending just before signing off, was nine hours per week. One-quarter were spending three or fewer hours a week studying, whilst 12 per cent were engaged for 30 hours or more. Eleven per cent undertook between 15 and 17 hours study. Women were more likely than men to be studying when unemployed. However, the biggest differences were linked to occupational status and previous qualifications: 28 per cent of professional people, for example, were studying while signing on (or just prior to signing off) compared to ten per cent of manual workers.

A majority (56 per cent) of respondents, and 80 per cent of those who were engaged in studying while unemployed, believed that study would assist them to obtain full-time work. Indeed, 52 per cent of those who were not undertaking study thought that it would have helped them. Further research, and the Workskill pilots, will aim to ascertain how employment prospects are affected by studying whilst claiming.

8 Routes off benefit   A principal aim of Jobseeker's Allowance policy is to stimulate a faster outflow from unemployment. In practice, under the Unemployment Benefit/Income Support system, 20 per cent of respondents managed this in the comparatively short period between sampling and conducting the interviews (Chapter 8.1).

Moving off benefit prior   The propensity to move off benefit prior to interview varied according to
to interview   claimant circumstances. More women left benefit than men at all ages (28 per cent overall compared to 18 per cent), and younger claimants, particularly those aged under 25, were more likely to leave benefit than most. The presence of children in the household did not affect the chances of a man leaving benefit but women with children aged five or more were more likely to sign off than those with younger children or without children. In general, more professional people had signed off by the time of interview than was the case for other occupational groups, but those men who were formerly managers appeared to have much more difficulty.

Most of those who had signed off by the time of interview had moved into paid employment. Fifty per cent of these went into full-time work and a further 11 per cent into part-time work with sufficient hours to disqualify most from receiving benefit. The other main destination was training, most commonly Training for Work. A marked gender difference was evident with women being more likely than men to move into part-time employment, whilst the opposite was true with regard to full-time employment.

Claimants' destination after leaving benefit was dependent on their age. Younger claimants were more likely to move into full-time work, whilst those aged 45 and over tended more often to go into part-time employment. Likewise, comparatively large numbers of the young, notably those aged under 25, took up full-time education, mainly for vocational training. A higher proportion of older claimants ceased looking for work due to ill health.

The most common source of information for those who found a job was a friend or relative (29 per cent) but other sources included a local paper (15 per cent), a Jobcentre (13 per cent) or a direct approach to an employer (12 per cent). The jobs taken were predominantly low-skilled, a third were temporary and another sixth of fixed duration. Less than half were permanent.

Problems leaving benefit   The transition from benefit to work is not always straightforward and, as noted above (Chapter 6.4), many respondents held reservations about such a move. Half of those who left benefit for employment did not encounter any difficulties but the others experienced a range of problems which closely echoed the fears of those still on benefit (Chapter 8.2). Financial difficulties were the most common problem, with many respondents suffering particular concern about delays receiving wages, paying the rent and incurring additional travelling expenses. Some groups reported more problems than others. For example, men seemed to encounter more difficulties than women, and those at either end of the age spectrum faced more problems than those aged in-between these extremes.

A long-standing policy concern has been the fear that some claimants have little incentive to sign off benefit because they are likely to be worse off in work. In reality three-fifths of the respondents who had already found work said they were better off in work although a fifth did feel that they were worse off.[1] Men were more likely than women to find themselves better off in work as were those who moved into full-time work. Similarly, a larger proportion of respondents without children reported that they gained financially as a consequence of finding a job than people with younger children. Finally, respondents returning to work after a comparatively short spell of less than six months on benefit were also more likely to feel themselves to be better off in work than those who had been out of work for longer.

Statistical analysis of 'spells'   Later stages of the research will concentrate upon determining how long people remain on benefit and the factors that are associated with the length of claim. At this stage, however, only a preliminary analysis was possible. This revealed that, for the sample of all claimants, those who were still unemployed had been out of work for an average of 58 weeks to date (Chapter 8.3). Preliminary modelling of spell lengths for the flow sample suggests that the average length of time that new claimants may expect to remain unemployed is 30 weeks. However, the comparatively small number of long spells was sufficient to bias this estimate upwards with an alternative statistic indicating that one-half of new claimants should have left unemployment within 21 weeks.

9 Conclusions   This report is based on the first of four national surveys of unemployed people, being conducted to evaluate Jobseeker's Allowance. It has aimed to establish key baseline statistics. At the same time it has highlighted areas where Jobseeker's Allowance will face greater and lesser obstacles to its successful implementation.

Unemployed people   The findings are largely consistent with existing information. Unemployed people tend to be from less skilled occupations, and to have limited formal

---

1   The fact that this minority had actually left benefit, despite being worse off, may indicate that financial gain is only one reason why people work. Equally, their experience this time might affect their future behaviour.

educational qualifications. New claimants are better qualified, suggesting they will leave benefit more quickly. Almost half of recent claimants (46 per cent) had never been unemployed before.

Job-search and other activities Claimants were not familiar with the details of the rules governing benefits. However most got on with the business of looking for work, without the threat of sanctions being a motivating factor. The removal of automatic access to Hardship Payments under Jobseeker's Allowance may alter perceptions of sanctions, and their effectiveness, and perhaps affect jobseeking behaviour. Moreover the new Jobseeker's Agreement may sharpen the focus on the rules governing entitlement to benefits.

Most claimants were looking for work, and were flexible about jobs with varying or unsocial working hours. However half had experienced periods when they temporarily stopped looking for work, and only minorities would consider either moving or working away from home. Those in areas of high unemployment were prepared to be more flexible than the average. Again, Jobseeker's Allowance will need to capitalise on existing areas of flexibility, and seek to discourage the type of temporary discouragement to which many claimants admit.

Obligations and rules Jobseeker's Allowance is designed to emphasise and enforce labour market obligations for unemployed claimants. In general terms, unemployed people knew they had to look for work and were content that penalties existed for claimants who did not. However awareness of the specifics of the rules was very general. Claimants often associated sanctions with fraud (undeclared earnings) rather than infringements of availability or actively seeking work. Those subject to sanctions were often taken by surprise – perhaps because it was for actions taken before they had even got to the Jobcentre, or because they had not fully understood the rules of the system when explained to them. Certainly, a sizeable proportion could not remember interviews they would have been expected to have, either at the start of claiming or at regular interviews thereafter.

The Back to Work Plan was often followed, at least in part. However the survey findings suggest a certain 'going through the motions' rather than practical benefits. The Jobseeker's Agreement should provide better-focused advice on the steps needed to comply with eligibility rules, and those likely to assist claimants in their job-search. By contrast 'active signing' procedures seemed more likely to affect claimant behaviour, but (at the time of the survey in September/October 1995) were patchily implemented.

1 THE DESIGN OF THE JOBSEEKER'S ALLOWANCE EVALUATION

Overview   This chapter aims to place the report in context. It briefly describes the main features of Jobseeker's Allowance, highlighting the nature of, and reasons for, changes to the system (Section 1.1). This is followed by a discussion of the main methodological considerations underlying the research, the research design, and the sampling (Section 1.2). The chapter closes by outlining the structure of the report (Section 1.3).

1.1 Jobseeker's Allowance   Jobseeker's Allowance was introduced on 7 October 1996,[1] replacing Unemployment Benefit and Income Support for unemployed people. It is a major policy reform, intended to increase the emphasis on benefit receipt from a passive consequence of unemployment to a more active effort to find work. It is the latest in a series of labour market reforms designed to increase the efficiency of the labour market, improve the skills of the workforce and encourage people in their job-search.

1.1.1 Objectives of Jobseeker's Allowance   The White Paper proposing Jobseeker's Allowance cited three main objectives:

1   To improve the operation of the labour market by helping people in their search for work, while ensuring that they understand and fulfil the conditions for receipt of benefit

2   To secure better value for money for the taxpayer by a streamlined administration, closer targeting on those who need financial support and a regime which more effectively helps people back into work

3   To improve the service to unemployed people themselves by a simpler, clearer, more consistent structure, and by better service delivery (Employment Department/Department of Social Security, 1994, page 5).

Jobseeker's Allowance is designed to encourage long-term claimants back into work and to ensure that the risk of short-term claimants becoming long-term claimants is reduced. To achieve this there are a number of new initiatives, including the Jobseeker's Agreement, Jobseeker's Direction and the Back to Work Bonus, discussed below.

1.1.2 What changes has Jobseeker's Allowance introduced?   Under the pre-Jobseeker's Allowance system, potential claimants had to meet a range of conditions. Some applied to Unemployment Benefit *and* Income Support, but each benefit also had separate rules. The most important included:

---

1   The rules are set out in the Jobseeker's Act 1995 and the Jobseeker's Allowance Regulations.

1

For both Unemployment Benefit and Income Support

- Being available for work (hours not specified)

- Actively seeking work.

For Unemployment Benefit

- Meeting conditions relating to National Insurance contributions[2]

- Benefit was assessed daily: no benefit was paid for a day if more than £2 was earned, and no benefit was paid in a week where more than £61 was earned

- Payment was at a flat-rate for those below pension age (there is a higher rate for those older than, but within five years of, pension age).

For Income Support

- Having income (including earnings) and capital below specified amounts

- Benefit was assessed weekly: claimants must be out of work or working fewer than 16 hours per week

- Payment was lower for those younger than 25 years.

Although Unemployment Benefit and Income Support have been replaced by a single structure (Jobseeker's Allowance), it has two components reflecting the previous system. The rules have been broadly aligned with those of Income Support. **Contribution-based Jobseeker's Allowance** is a 'social insurance' benefit that replaced Unemployment Benefit, whilst **income-based Jobseeker's Allowance** replaced Income Support for the unemployed. The conditions for eligibility remain, with contribution-based Jobseeker's Allowance awarded to those with sufficient National Insurance contributions, and income-based Jobseeker's Allowance awarded to those who are ineligible for the contributory benefit and/or whose income and capital are below specific amounts.

Following the introduction of Jobseeker's Allowance, claimants have additional obligations. The labour market conditions are stricter, with claimants having to sign a 'Jobseeker's Agreement' as a condition of benefit receipt. This Agreement replaces the Back to Work Plan previously completed by new claimants. It is a personal agreement detailing the steps each individual intends to take to find employment. However whilst the Back to Work Plan was an advisory and voluntary document, the Jobseeker's Agreement is a condition of benefit receipt and expresses other conditions on which benefit entitlement depends. The Agreement will enable staff to

---

2 Claimants must have paid Class 1 contributions on earnings 25 times the lower earnings limit in *either* of the two complete tax years before the start of the benefit year in which the claim is made, and in *each* of these must have paid or been credited with contributions on earnings 50 times the lower earnings limit.

monitor activities. This monitoring responds to a concern in the White Paper that *'the longer people stay on benefit the more their motivation and skills may decline'*. By making jobseeking activity a condition of benefit receipt, it is intended to sustain claimants' motivation to find employment. However, failure to carry out all of the activities in the Agreement will not, necessarily lead to a sanction, if claimants can show they met the availability and actively seeking work conditions in the weeks in question.

Under Jobseeker's Allowance, Employment Service advisers can issue a Jobseeker's Direction. This takes the form of a written requirement to claimants that they adopt certain reasonable measures to improve their chances of employment by:

> *'attending a course to improve jobseeking skills or motivation, or taking steps to present themselves acceptably to employers.'*
>
> *(Employment Department/Department of Social Security, 1994)*

It will be used where it is felt that a claimant requires help looking for work, or where there are doubts about a claimant's commitment to look for work.

The duration of benefit has also changed. Eligible claimants were able to receive Unemployment Benefit for up to 12 months, but the contribution-based Jobseeker's Allowance is available for, at most, six months. After the six months have expired, claimants may become entitled to income-based Jobseeker's Allowance. In addition, some claimants may receive income-based Jobseeker's Allowance when they get contributory Jobseeker's Allowance if, for example, they are supporting other members of a family such as children or a non-working partner.

There are transitional arrangements from April 1996. The general rule governing entitlement to transitional protection in Jobseeker's Allowance is that Unemployment Benefit and/or Income Support (as an unemployed person) must be payable (or treated as payable) for the point of change to Jobseeker's Allowance, i.e. on 5/6 October 1996. The components which are protected include: general cash protection for all contribution-based claimants; dependency increases which were payable on 5/6 October; the Unemployment Benefit age limit for claimants with an occupational or personal pension, i.e. only those over 55; and the Unemployment Benefit earnings rules.

The duration of contribution-based benefit is also protected. Where Unemployment Benefit was payable for the 6/7 April 1996, *and* remained payable for 5/6 October 1996, *and* there was no break in benefit for more than eight weeks between these dates, jobseekers are entitled to a maximum of 312 days' entitlement to contributory benefit. If Unemployment Benefit was not payable for the 6/7 April 1996, the maximum entitlement under Jobseeker's Allowance is 156 days. Therefore, if on 7 October a customer had already received 156 days' benefit or more, their contribution-based benefit would cease. If not, they would receive the balance as contribution-based Jobseeker's Allowance. Transitional protection ceases in April 1997.

An additional component of Jobseeker's Allowance, available after three months' of unemployment, is the Back to Work Bonus. According to the Jobseeker's Allowance White Paper, this is designed to '*reward individuals and their partners who take part-time work whilst receiving Jobseeker's Allowance, and will provide them with a greater incentive to move into employment of 16 hours or more*'. Although levels of benefit are reduced for any amount in excess of disregarded earnings from part-time work, half of earnings above this limit are credited to the claimant's bonus scheme. This will accumulate until the claimant increases their hours of work or earnings sufficiently to take them off benefit. It is paid in a tax-free lump sum upon finding employment.[3] The Bonus is available to all Jobseeker's Allowance claimants and Income Support claimants under the age of 60.

1.1.3 Sanctions   Under the Unemployment Benefit/Income Support system, those failing the basic labour market requirements for benefit receipt may have had their benefit disallowed (i.e. stopped). Sanctions, taking the form of a benefit penalty, could also be imposed upon those who unreasonably caused or perpetuated their unemployment. This would apply to those who, for example, turn down a job offer without good cause. Those who had sanctions imposed could have received a hardship allowance for the duration of the penalty, incurring a penalty of 40 per cent of the Income Support personal rate.

Under Jobseeker's Allowance, the basic penalties remain but the rules governing them have been clarified and sharpened. The new system is more stringent due to the revised labour market conditions for benefit receipt. Claimants who are not available for work, fail actively to seek work, fail to sign a Jobseeker's Agreement or who do not attend an Employment Service interview are disallowed benefit until they fulfil the relevant condition.

Jobseeker's Allowance carries forward many elements of the previous system. For instance, those who leave a job voluntarily or turn down a job offer without good cause will have a sanction imposed that could last for as long as six months. Shorter sanctions will be imposed upon those who fail to attend mandatory courses, such as Jobplan Workshops or prescribed training courses, or who do not act upon their Jobseeker's Directions. This disqualification will be for two weeks, but increased to four weeks if repeated within 12 months.

1.1.4 Hardship payments   There are also changes to the rules governing receipt of hardship allowance: the new system does not offer automatic payments to those sanctioned. Instead, the onus is on the claimant to demonstrate that '*a member of the household would suffer hardship as a result*' of a sanction being imposed. If a

---

3 Up to a maximum of £1,000.

hardship allowance is awarded, it will not be available for the first two weeks of sanction (except for those deemed to be 'vulnerable'), but the level of payment will be as under the previous system. Hardship payments may be made at the start of a claim or in the course of a claim which is referred to an Adjudication Officer. Those in vulnerable groups can also receive hardship payments following a decision to disallow benefit over a labour market question.

1.1.5 Jobseeker's Allowance delivery

From the claimant's perspective, there should be a noticeable change in the administration and delivery of the benefit system. Rather than dealing with two separate offices (Employment Service for entitlement to Unemployment Benefit, and the Benefits Agency for Income Support) as before, Jobseeker's Allowance is delivered via Jobcentres by both Employment Service and Benefits Agency staff. The Jobcentre therefore provides:

> *'a single point of contact for jobseekers to receive help and advice on their search for jobs, to obtain access to a wide range of vacancies, training and employment programmes and to claim Jobseeker's Allowance.'*
>
> *(Employment Department/Department of Social Security, 1994)*

1.2 Rationale and research design

It is part of the requirement for all new government policies to set out what the policy aims to achieve and how the achievements will be measured. In 1995 the Centre for Research in Social Policy at Loughborough University was jointly commissioned by Department for Education and Employment, the Employment Service, the Benefits Agency and the Department of Social Security to conduct an evaluation of the Jobseeker's Allowance.

The evaluation takes the form of a 'before-and-after' study in which the benefit world after the introduction of Jobseeker's Allowance is compared with the previous system. Each 'cohort' in fact comprises both an inflow and a stock sample. This report concerns only the first wave of the pre-Jobseeker's Allowance cohort. **The principal objective of this report is to establish *part* of the baseline.** Subsequent measures, taken at the second wave, and also following the implementation of Jobseeker's Allowance, may then be compared. The overall baseline is provided by the whole pre-Jobseeker's Allowance sample: not only the first wave on which this report is based.

1.2.1 Research objectives

This research project has a number of objectives. It is designed to provide an understanding of the determinants of transitions identified through macroeconomic and statistical analysis.

This report forms part of the 'baselines' against which the effectiveness of Jobseeker's Allowance may be assessed. This will enable the impact of Jobseeker's Allowance to be compared against its objectives and sub-objectives. The baseline is designed to capture those factors affecting the behaviour of unemployed claimants in the labour market. There are two waves, enabling us to measure claimant behaviour over a six-month period, and to relate that behaviour to claimant characteristics, the local labour market and to Employment Service interventions.

The baseline information provides the most up-to-date picture of unemployed claimants under the Unemployment Benefit/Income Support regime that prevailed prior to October 1996. It provides detailed data on claimants' attitudes and responses to Employment Service advice, information on the positions of various different groups of the unemployed, and on those factors appearing to affect the behaviour of unemployed claimants.

1.2.2 Research design The research is designed to detect and measure the types of changes anticipated from the introduction of Jobseeker's Allowance and to identify the factors which contribute to this change. The research design adopted is a variation of the classic 'before-and-after' design in which two separate independent samples, one drawn before and the other after an intervention (i.e. the introduction of Jobseeker's Allowance), are compared and any changes observed. It will be important to separate changes due to Jobseeker's Allowance *policy* from the changes due to *delivery* of Jobseeker's Allowance, and in turn to separate these from overall economic effects.

The pre-Jobseeker's Allowance surveys are referred to as 'Cohort 1', consisting of 'Wave 1' and 'Wave 2'. The post-Jobseeker's Allowance world, 'Cohort 2', will be recorded by two similar waves. In both cases, details of respondents' claiming history and work history over a period of two years prior to the Wave 1 survey are gathered on 'Work Benefit History sheets'.

1.2.3 Timetable Figure 1.1 indicates the approximate timetable for the research. The sample for the first wave of the first cohort was drawn in July/August 1995 and the interviews conducted in September, October and November 1995. Interviews for the second wave of the first cohort began six months later in March 1996 and were completed at the beginning of June. As far as possible, individual respondents were interviewed six months after their initial interview and were staggered so that each claimant had an interval of six months between their first and second interview.

1.2.4 Sampling The system of sampling ensured that:

- the sample reflected the characteristics of the caseload of unemployed

- there were enough 'new' and existing claims

- there were sufficient numbers of interviews with less common groups.

Much of this report, and the analysis it contains, relies on the concepts of the stock and flow of the unemployed. The stock was drawn from those unemployed for at least two weeks, whilst the flow were selected because they had been signing on for less than two weeks.

Figure 1.1   The research design

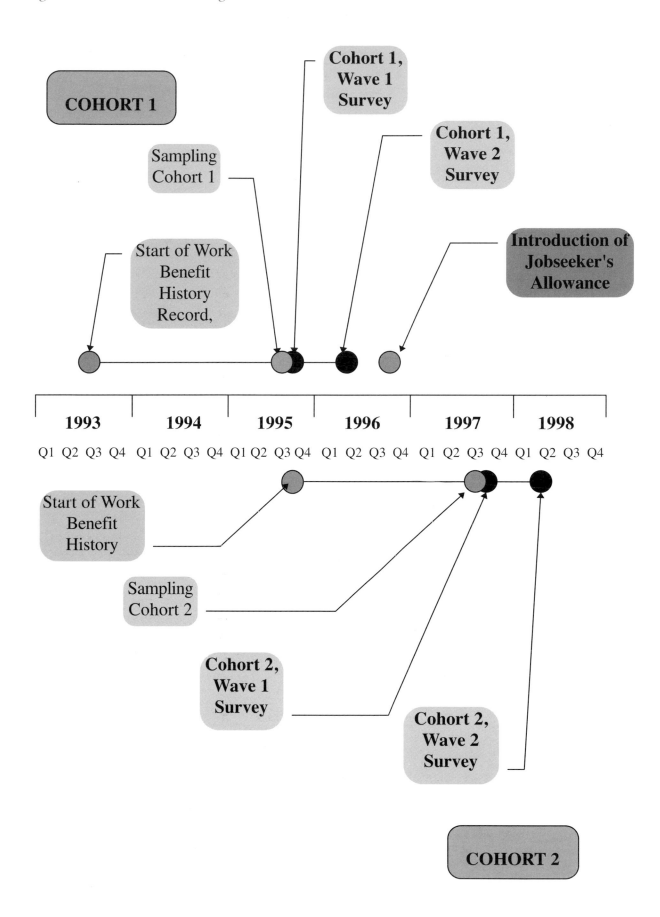

These two samples may be combined to produce a representative cross-section of those unemployed at the time of sampling. This requires that the flow be given a suitable 'weighting' in the analysis. However it is sometimes appropriate to look separately at the stock and the flow.

Analysts have sometimes used a number of analogies to convey the key distinction between stock and flow. Perhaps the key point is that whilst all of the stock were once 'inflow', over time selective exits and ageing mean that the stock begins to look quite different from the flow. If we think about a health club, many people may join, but the characteristics of new members may not resemble the stock of current members. That is because some people are more likely to leave ('selective exit'), because people may change over time ('ageing'), and lastly because the characteristics of people joining today may be quite different from those who joined last year, or the year before. Perhaps a 'health craze' led to a large inflow in a particular year.

The situation is similar with unemployment. Some of the newly unemployed will leave more quickly than others; remaining unemployed may itself actually change people's characteristics; and the inflow may vary with the condition of the economic cycle. One year it may be manufacturing workers becoming unemployed; the next there might be greater 'white collar' unemployment.

It was important to ensure that the sample accurately reflected the characteristics of the claimant caseload at the relevant point in time. However, as a main objective was to focus attention on both the unemployed stock at a point in time and new claimants, the sampling strategy adopted had to reflect this. Simply taking a sample of those unemployed at a point in time would have meant a disproportionately large sample of longer term claimants. It would also have been more difficult to establish attitudes and behaviour patterns for those at the point of entry to the system (known as the 'flow' of claimants) due to the relatively small numbers of new claimants in the stock. It was therefore decided to aim for a sample containing equal numbers of new and existing claimants, as defined by the duration of claim.

Further distinctions may be made according to the type of benefit received by claimants. Without disproportionate sampling fractions, a very large sample of Income Support claimants would be generated, but very few receiving, for example, both Income Support and Unemployment Benefit. A disproportionate stratification method was adopted that differentially sampled within groups, defined by the type of benefit received, to ensure that sufficient cases were available for each of these analytical subgroups. These groups consisted of claimants receiving: Income Support; Unemployment Benefit; both Income Support and Unemployment Benefit; or neither Income Support nor Unemployment Benefit. This last group consists of those receiving National Insurance credits and those who are in receipt of nothing at the time of sampling, possibly as a result of an unprocessed claim. A representative sample was achieved by applying weights to cases according to their benefit group and the duration of their claim. The samples were drawn from the National Unemployment Benefit System and claimants were selected from 100 Employment Service local offices around the country. Full details of the weighting strategy and precise nature of the sampling can be found in Appendix A. Further methodological details, together with the questionnaires and other documents used in the survey, can be found in a separate technical report (Nove, 1997).

A final consideration concerned those cases held as 'clerical' records. These typically represent more complex cases and usually result from problems with claims such as a missing National Insurance number. A small sample of these claimants whose records were clerically held was therefore taken from some offices.

1.3 Organisation of the report

The remainder of this report presents analyses based on the first wave of the first cohort survey. The results therefore describe the characteristics, experiences and behaviour of unemployed claimants before the introduction of Jobseeker's Allowance. Findings from the second wave survey will generate information on the length of time for which unemployed people claim benefit, and document any changes in attitudes or behaviour that occur as the duration of a person's claim increases, and will be covered in a separate report.

The results are important both in themselves, relating as they do to what is probably the largest and most detailed survey of the experiences of unemployed claimants and their families ever conducted in Britain, and especially for what they reveal about the potential of Jobseeker's Allowance to stimulate real change in the attitudes and behaviour of unemployed claimants. Therefore, particular attention is paid, notably in Chapters 4, 5, 6 and 7, to aspects of claimants' experience that are predicted to change with the introduction of Jobseeker's Allowance and to identify factors that may either facilitate or hinder the successful implementation of the new scheme.

The remainder of this report analyses various aspects of the survey. Chapter 2 presents a variety of descriptions of the respondents, paying particular attention to contrasts between new and all claimants. Chapter 3 deals with claimants' work experience prior to their most recent spell of signing on and how they came to be unemployed. Eligibility for receipt of benefit is contingent upon certain criteria and Chapter 4 deals with respondents' understanding of the rules for signing on, as well as their understanding and experience of disqualifications and disallowances. In Chapter 5, the claimants' experience of dealing with the Employment Service and Benefits Agency is explored. A main objective of Jobseeker's Allowance is to encourage job-search activities, and Chapter 6 considers what claimants were doing to find work, the intensity of these activities and their expectations. Chapter 7 is concerned with other activities that respondents may be doing whilst claiming benefit, such as part-time work, education or voluntary work. Jobseeker's Allowance aims to facilitate the outflow from unemployment and Chapter 8 describes the previous system in terms of movements off benefit, claimants' destinations and indicates which groups are most likely to move off. Finally, Chapter 9 provides a number of conclusions.

2 CLAIMANT CHARACTERISTICS

Overview This chapter provides an introduction to the characteristics of the unemployed, and represents the most up-to-date and detailed information available. It describes the respondents to the survey, focusing on the similarities and differences between recent and all claimants. It is, inevitably, more descriptive and contains rather more tables than the chapters in the remainder of the report.

Throughout this report, the terms 'flow' and 'stock' are used to refer to certain claimant groups. The flow represents new claimants, that is those entering the system no more than two weeks prior to sampling. The stock is a cross-section through the entire claimant population at the time of sampling and includes a range of signing durations, from recent additions to the register to those who have been signing on for many years.

Some of the flow will have managed to sign off fairly quickly, whilst others will still be signing on at the time of interview and will remain in the system for an unknown length of time. Some of the stock, though a smaller proportion, will also have signed off prior to interview.

The following sections examine:

- the number of interviews achieved, and the weighting process adopted (Section 2.1)

- the social and demographic characteristics of claimants and their families (Section 2.2)

- recent history of signing on and benefit receipt (Section 2.3)

- details of economic activity (Section 2.4)

- information, where relevant, about partners (Section 2.5).

2.1 Interviews achieved and weighting The sample was selected to produce a fully representative cross-section of those signing on at the time of the survey, whilst interviewing enough people in particular circumstances where a random sample would have contained too few cases. Weights were applied to achieve representativeness, and to compensate for different response rates. Appendix A contains full details of the weighting procedure used. The weighted sample, as discussed in this report, refers to the sample as it most closely resembles the population of those signing on.

Table 2.1 shows the sample sizes and proportions for the total stock of claimants (i.e. stock and flow samples combined), with and without weighting. A distinction is made between those who had been signing on for less than two weeks at the time of sampling and those signing on for longer, the latter further divided by the type of benefit received. **Subsequent mention of the stock of claimants refers to the weighted sample** as shown in Table 2.1.

Table 2.1   Unweighted and weighted sample sizes for the total stock of claimants

Claimant category	Unweighted		Weighted	
	Number	Column per cent	Number	Column per cent
Clericals	49	1	–	–
Signing on for less than 2 weeks	2,387	49	250	5
Signing on for more than 2 weeks				
Income Support	1,048	22	3,047	64
Unemployment Benefit	560	12	629	13
Income Support and Unemployment				
Benefit	365	8	237	5
Neither Income Support nor				
Unemployment Benefit	467	10	570	12
Total	4,876	100	4,732	100

– = true zero

The unweighted sample size of 4,876 represents a 75 per cent response rate from the issued sample. Approximately one-half (49 per cent) of the sample were people who had been signing on for less than two weeks. This relatively high proportion was collected to ensure that sufficient numbers were available for more sophisticated statistical analysis of the destinations of the flow, and the time spent on benefit, and to investigate the role of new claims procedures. However, for the purposes of describing the unemployed as a group, these cases are allocated a small weight and thus account for just over five per cent of the weighted stock sample.

Some analyses in the following sections will concentrate on the flow. On these occasions, the sample of those signing on for less than two weeks is weighted to compensate for different response rates (see Appendix A), giving a total flow sample size of 2,431 cases.

The other major change as a result of the weighting is the 'boosting' of the numbers of those signing on for longer than two weeks and receiving Income Support. Although only 22 per cent of responses were obtained from these individuals, they represent over 60 per cent of the claimant population. The remaining categories do not alter drastically from weighting.

The survey also included 49 'clerical cases' (representing one per cent of all responses). These are, typically, more complex benefit claims and are deliberately excluded from the weighted stock and flow samples. Separate analysis of this group will be conducted in the second report on the whole pre-Jobseeker's Allowance sample, using data from both waves. However the small sample size precludes detailed analysis.

2.2 Social and demographic characteristics of claimants

The characteristics of survey respondents will be described in this section. Comparisons will be made between the stock and flow to highlight differences between those signing on more recently, and claimants in general. The latter group, predominantly those who have claimed for longer than two weeks, are likely to represent those who find it more difficult to return to work or some other economic activity, and who thus 'accumulate' within the system.

2.2.1 Gender

A third (34 per cent) of those newly unemployed were women and 66 per cent were men (see Figure 2.1). This compares with 37 per cent and 63 per cent respectively in 1987 (Garman, Redmond and Lonsdale, 1992).

Figure 2.1   Gender of respondents

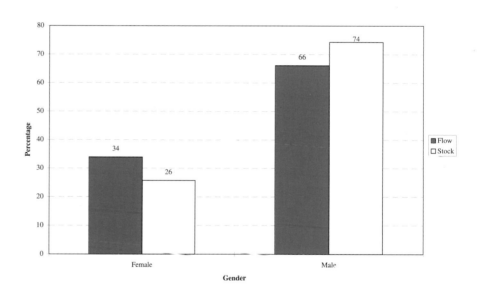

The stock, however, contained a rather higher proportion of men (74 per cent). The comparison with the flow suggests that there is a tendency for men to find it more difficult to move back into employment (or another activity) than women. This tends to reflect current trends in the labour market, where the main area of decline is male employment, particularly among the unskilled (Gregg, 1993).

2.2.2 Age

Those in the stock sample were, on average, two years older than those in the flow. The mean age of the flow was 32.2 years (standard deviation = 12.2), compared with 34.1 years for the stock (standard deviation = 12.1).

The implication is that slightly older people are less able to sign off within a short space of time than those unemployed at younger ages. The age distributions for both types of claimants are shown in Figures 2.2a and 2.2b.

Figure 2.2a   Age distribution for flow

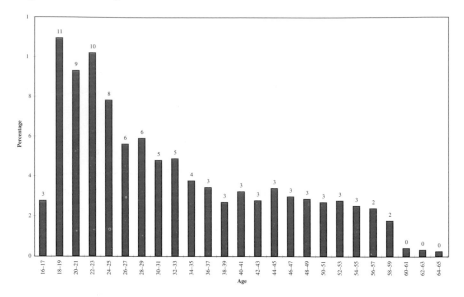

Figure 2.2b   Age distribution for stock

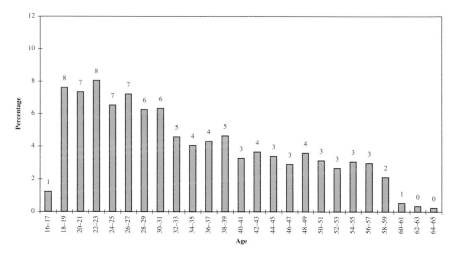

In general terms, the age distribution among respondents peaks during the early twenties, with a gradual fall in numbers for older groups. The most notable difference between the two distributions is the more pronounced 'peak' at the younger end of the scale, followed by a more rapid decline, for the flow respondents. Whilst the ages of the stock of respondents peaks at around the same age (20 to 25 years), the decline in numbers is more gradual. This confirms the slight tendency for older claimants to be more likely to remain in the stock rather than find a route off.

Table 2.2 outlines the household composition for the flow and stock samples. For ease of interpretation, no distinction is made between households with different numbers of children, and the specification of each category refers to the youngest child in that household irrespective of the presence of any older children. The categories are mutually exclusive and are designed to show the most appropriate household characteristic.

The most common household type, for both new (34 per cent) and all (27 per cent) claimants, was living with parents. Not surprisingly, the mean age for those in this category was among the lowest for any household group (23 years for the flow, 25 for the stock) suggesting that many of these claimants had not yet left home.

One of the biggest differences between new and existing claimants was in the proportion of those living alone. Sixteen per cent of the new claimants and one-quarter (24 per cent) of the stock of claimants were living alone. Thus, it appears that those living alone have a tendency to find it more difficult to sign off. A total of 897 (37 per cent) of the flow and 1,752 (37 per cent) of the stock lived with a partner. Interviews were obtained with 1,313 of these partners (75 per cent), who are described in Section 2.5. Of those with partners, 62 per cent of the flow and 73 per cent of the stock had children. Around three per cent of both the flow and stock were lone parents.

Table 2.2   Household composition

Household type	Flow		Stock	
	Number	Column per cent	Number	Column per cent
Lives alone	394	16	1,178	24
Partner and no children	344	14	481	10
Partner and child under 5	227	9	608	13
Partner and child 5–15	212	9	453	10
Partner and child 16+	114	5	210	4
Single parent – child under 5, no other children	5	*	11	*
Single parent – child 5–15, no other children	15	*	19	*
Single parent – child 16+, no other children	24	1	69	2
Single parent – child under 5, other children	2	*	10	*
Single parent – child 5–15, other children	2	*	6	*
Single parent – child 16+, other children	13	1	17	*
Lives with parent(s)	824	34	1,266	27
Lives with other relative	77	3	175	4
Lives with non-relatives	179	7	280	6
Total	2,431		4,732	

* = less than 0.5 per cent, more than zero

There was little difference in the marital status of new and existing claimants, as shown in Table 2.3. The differences that are apparent (e.g. the higher proportion of single people and lower proportion of divorcees in the flow) can be mainly explained by other factors such as age.

Table 2.3   Relationship status

Relationship status	Flow		Stock	
	Number	Column per cent	Number	Column per cent
Married or living as married	902	37	1,751	37
Widowed	8	1	39	1
Divorced	153	6	408	9
Separated	77	3	184	4
Single	1,279	53	2,342	50
Total[1]	2,419		4,724	

Around two-fifths of lone parents (43 per cent of the flow, 39 per cent of the stock) were divorced, whilst a further 21 per cent of the flow and 29 per cent of the stock described their marital status as separated. An additional one-quarter (27 per cent in the flow, 26 per cent in the stock) of lone parents were single, never married.

2.2.4 Ethnic group   The majority of respondents were white (91 per cent of the new claimants and 89 per cent of the stock) as illustrated in Table 2.4.

Table 2.4   Ethnic group

Ethnic group	Flow		Stock	
	Number	Column per cent	Number	Column per cent
White	2,205	91	4,198	89
Black African	32	1	61	1
Black Caribbean	33	1	105	2
Black other	15	1	24	1
Indian	43	2	82	2
Pakistani	34	1	85	2
Bangladeshi	24	1	55	1
Chinese	5	*	4	*
Other	25	1	81	2
Prefer not to say	5	*	24	1
Total[1]	2,421		4,720	

* = less than 0.5 per cent, more than zero

---

1   Note that totals less than 2,431 for the flow and 4,372 for the stock indicate missing values.

The other groups typically represented just one or two per cent of claimants, with little difference between the flow and stock. There is therefore no evidence to suggest that claimants belonging to some ethnic groups are any more likely to accumulate in the system than others: however the follow-up data will provide a clearer picture. This is initial evidence between ethnic group and the duration of unemployment. However, evidence from the Labour Force Survey does suggest that whites are less likely to become unemployed than people from ethnic minority backgrounds (Jones, 1993).

2.2.5 Social class 'Social class' groupings were based on the respondents' regular jobs or, in cases where no regular job was mentioned, their previous jobs. Table 2.5 shows the number and proportion of respondents in different social classes for the flow and stock. The category 'no regular job described' relates to those who have worked in a variety of jobs, but never spent sufficient time in any one profession to consider it 'regular'.

Table 2.5   Social class

Social class	Flow		Stock	
	Number	Column per cent	Number	Column per cent
Professional	60	3	91	2
Managerial/technical	514	22	954	21
Skilled non-manual	478	20	656	14
Skilled manual	502	21	1,047	23
Partly skilled	427	18	876	19
Unskilled	162	7	424	9
Never worked	177	7	366	8
Armed forces	14	*	34	*
No regular job described	57	2	183	4
Total	2,391		4,630	

* = less than 0.5 per cent, more than zero

Most (80 per cent) respondents were in one of four social classes: managerial or technical (II), skilled non-manual (IIIM), skilled manual (IIIN) and partly skilled (IV). These categories accounted for a roughly equal number of new claimants (each about 20 per cent). The stock sample contained proportionally fewer skilled non-manual workers, suggesting that members of this group tend to find it slightly easier to sign off. This reflects the gradual change in emphasis from manual to non-manual work in manufacturing over the past few decades (Machin, 1993, cited in Balls and Gregg, 1993). In contrast, unskilled ex-workers were more prevalent in the stock, indicating that they tend to find it more difficult to sign off than other classes. Unsurprisingly, this was also true for those who had not worked sufficiently regularly to be classified.

2.2.6 Qualifications There were differences in the level and type of qualifications held by the flow and stock samples, as shown in Figure 2.3, and described in this section.

Figure 2.3   Vocational and academic qualifications

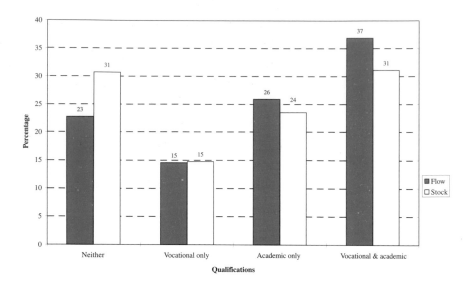

Twenty-three per cent of the flow sample had neither vocational nor academic qualifications, but more of the stock (31 per cent) were unqualified. Research conducted in 1987 (Garman, Redmond and Lonsdale, 1992) indicated that 32 per cent of the flow lacked qualifications of any type, indicating that more of the newly unemployed are qualified than eight years previously, although the proportion of school-leavers with qualifications has also risen over this time.

Equal proportions (15 per cent) of the flow and stock samples had vocational, but no academic, qualifications. Slightly more flow respondents (26 per cent) had academic qualifications than those in the stock (24 per cent), but there was a bigger difference in the proportion with both types of qualification. Thirty-seven per cent of the flow had at least one vocational qualification in conjunction with academic qualifications, whilst 31 per cent of the stock had both types of qualification. Although, on the face of it, this suggests a tendency for those with qualifications to find it easier to sign off, no significant difference was found between the qualifications held by flow and stock respondents.

Having described the numbers with qualifications, we now look at those qualifications in more detail.

a)   Vocational qualifications
Fifty-two per cent of the flow had at least one vocational qualification, compared with just 46 per cent of the stock. Table 2.6 shows the numbers and proportions in possession of vocational qualifications.

For vocational qualifications, the differences between the new and existing claimants were mostly small and not statistically significant. The single most common vocational qualification held was the City & Guilds Part 1, held by 13 per cent of the flow and 12 per cent of the stock. Those who had undertaken a National Vocational Qualification (NVQ) were asked to report the highest level completed. Of the flow respondents with NVQs, 22 per cent were qualified to Level 1, 53 per cent to Level 2, 13 per cent to Level 3, four per cent to Level 4 and just under half a per cent to Level 5. The equivalent for the stock of claimants were not substantially different, with 25 per cent, 46 per cent, 15 per cent, three per cent and one per cent qualified to NVQ Levels 1 to 5 respectively (this is a statistically significant difference). An additional eight per cent of the flow and ten per cent of the stock did not know the highest level of their NVQ.

Table 2.6   Vocational qualifications[3]

Vocational qualification	Flow		Stock	
	Number	Column per cent	Number	Column per cent
Trade apprenticeship	127	5	191	4
City & Guilds: Part 1	307	13	553	12
City & Guilds: Part 2/3	217	9	356	8
City & Guilds: Not known	107	5	225	5
BTEC or equivalent	152	6	233	5
ONC/OND/SCOTVEC National	161	7	283	6
HNC/HND/SCOTVEC Higher	109	5	204	4
Pitman's/RSA	206	9	319	7
Other clerical/commercial qualification	61	3	95	2
NVQ/SVQ	205	9	441	9
GNVQ/GSVQ	32	1	42	1
Other vocational	201	8	321	7
None	1,163	49	2,530	54
Base	2,397		4,669	

b)   *Academic qualifications*

There was little difference between the flow and stock in school leaving age. For both samples, the average leaving age was 16.2 years (standard deviation 1.3) and the median 16 years. However, 31 per cent of the new claimants left school after 16, whereas this was true of 27 per cent of the stock. After leaving school or sixth-form college, 35 per cent of the flow went on to do some full-time education compared with 29 per cent of the stock.

Academic qualifications (i.e. those with General Certificate of Secondary Education (GCSE) (or equivalent, grades D, E or F or above) were held by 63 per cent of the flow and 55 per cent of the stock (see Table 2.7).

3 Note that this table contains multiple response data as some respondents reported having two or more vocational qualifications. The column percentages are based upon the number of cases rather than responses and so do not sum to 100 per cent.

Table 2.7   Academic qualifications

Highest academic qualification	Flow		Stock	
	Number	Column per cent	Number	Column per cent
Degree or higher	275	11	396	8
'A' level or equivalent	199	8	381	8
'O' level pass or equivalent	683	28	1,134	24
CSE grade 2 or below or equivalent	313	13	556	12
Other	53	2	107	2
None	907	37	2,154	46
Total	2,429		4,727	

The difference between flow and stock respondents stems mainly from those qualified to degree level and those with at least one 'O' level pass. Eleven per cent of the flow were educated to at least degree level in contrast to eight per cent of the stock; whilst 28 per cent of the flow achieved 'O' level passes (or equivalents) yet this was true of 24 per cent of the stock.

Few respondents had difficulties with 'basic' skills. Most (91 per cent of new claimants; 88 per cent of the stock) had neither reading nor writing problems. However, four per cent of the flow and five per cent of the stock had a problem with both. A further one per cent of the flow and one per cent of the stock claimed a problem with reading; two and three per cent respectively had a problem with writing; and two and three per cent respectively qualified a stated reading or writing problem by indicating that English was not their first language. Almost five per cent of new claimants expressed some problem with numbers or simple arithmetic, as did seven per cent of the stock.

2.3 Signing on and benefit receipt
2.3.1 Signing duration

The length of time for which respondents had been claiming benefit was used to distinguish flow from stock. By definition, the flow would have been claiming benefit for no more than two weeks at the time of sampling. The descriptions contained in this section are of the stock, five per cent of whom had been claiming for less than two weeks.

The mean duration (according to Employment Service records) was 446 days,[4] or just under 15 months. However, the skewed nature of the durations is shown by the median value of 187 days (just over six months); a substantial proportion of individuals had been signing on for very long periods, as confirmed by Figure 2.4.

In very general terms, as claiming duration increases, the number of respondents decreases. The peak duration is between two weeks and three months, accounting for 28 per cent of respondents. The other peak at one to two years can be explained by the unequal increments between groupings

4   The standard deviation was 689 days. This is a measure of how varied the figures were: the top one in 40 would be expected to be the mean plus twice the standard deviation.

(this being the first to cover a 12 months period unlike the preceding ones which span just three months). The final category, representing those who have been signing on for over five years, contains around four per cent of respondents. The maximum value was 18 years (6,606 days).

Figure 2.4   Distribution of signing duration

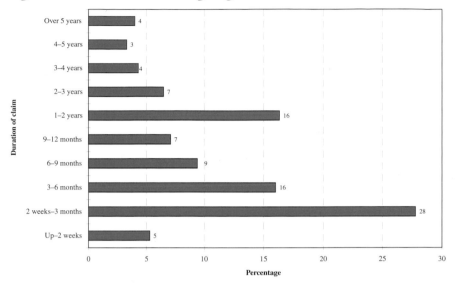

2.3.2 Benefit status at the time of interview

The interviews took place between two and three months after the sample was drawn. In this time, 36 per cent of the flow and 20 per cent of the stock had signed off. A further distinction can be made between those respondents whose signing spell (upon which they were selected for the sample) was their first or whether they were repeat claimers of benefit. Figure 2.5 shows the proportions of flow and stock respondents in each of these four possible benefit status categories.

The majority of respondents were still signing on at the time of interview. However, there were notable differences between flow and stock samples. Half (50 per cent) of the stock were 'current' claimants on their first spell of benefit receipt whilst this is true of just 30 per cent of the new claimants. Most of this difference is because more of the newer claimants had signed off by the interview. Respondents in the flow were also more likely to be repeat claimants than the stock (54 and 40 per cent respectively). This lends weight to the argument that many of the flow will be people who are more transient claimants, alternating between employment and unemployment on a more regular basis.

Figure 2.5   Benefit status

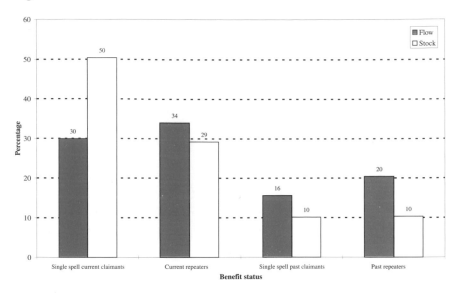

2.3.3 Benefit receipt
at the time of interview Figure 2.6 shows the proportion of those still signing on who were in receipt of each of the main types of benefit at the time of the interview. The figures will largely reflect the sampling and weighting processes applied to the data.

Figure 2.6   Receipt of unemployment linked benefits at interview

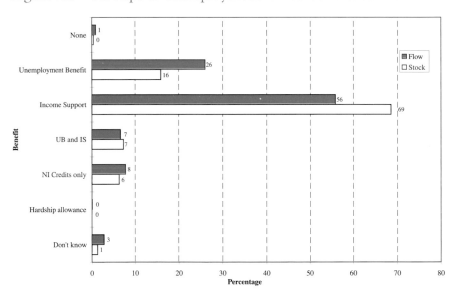

Income Support, claimed by 69 per cent of the existing claimants and 56 per cent of new claimants was the most common benefit. Unemployment Benefit was claimed as a single benefit by 26 per cent of the flow and 16 per cent of the stock. As claimants lost their entitlement to Unemployment Benefit after 12 months under the prevailing system, a smaller proportion of the stock (34 per cent of whom had been claiming for more than a year) claimed this benefit.

Around seven per cent of both stock and flow received Unemployment Benefit and Income Support and a slightly higher proportion of those in the flow (eight per cent) than the stock (six per cent) received National Insurance credits only. Fewer than one per cent of both new and existing claimants were in receipt of no benefits and a marginally greater proportion (two per cent of the flow, one per cent of the stock) did not know which benefit they received.

Respondents were also asked about benefits received (by the household) in addition to Income Support or Unemployment Benefit. A higher proportion of the stock (58 per cent) than the flow (43 per cent) claimed at least one other benefit; perhaps because some of the more recent claimants may not yet have applied for such benefits or not yet had their case reviewed. Housing Benefit was the single most commonly claimed benefit received by 26 per cent of the flow and 39 per cent of the stock. Around one-fifth claimed Child Benefit (18 per cent of new claimants and 23 per cent of the stock). However, most other benefits were received by only a small proportion of claimants.

2.3.4 Benefit receipt during the observation period

The 'Work Benefit History Sheet' was used to obtain information concerning respondents' economic activity and benefit claiming history over the two years prior to the interview. This may be referred to as the 'observation period'. No distinction is made between any of the different types of benefit, and the information recorded on a weekly basis simply distinguished between those receiving benefit, those claiming National Insurance credits only, and those claiming neither. This section provides a brief description of some of this information; Section 8.3 provides more detailed analysis.

The 'Work Benefit History Sheet' covered a substantial period of time. For those with several changes during this time, the dates might be thought to be potentially inaccurate. Interviewers were asked to record what proportion of dates were, in their estimation, accurate to within two weeks. In three-quarters of cases (74 per cent) interviewers said they believed that 'All or nearly all' met this standard. A further 15 per cent said that more than half were accurate to within two weeks. Most respondents claimed Income Support or Unemployment Benefit during the observation period and relatively few claimed only National Insurance credits. A small proportion (six per cent) claimed both benefit and National Insurance credits at some point.

Figure 2.7   Observation period spent claiming benefit (not 'National Insurance Only')

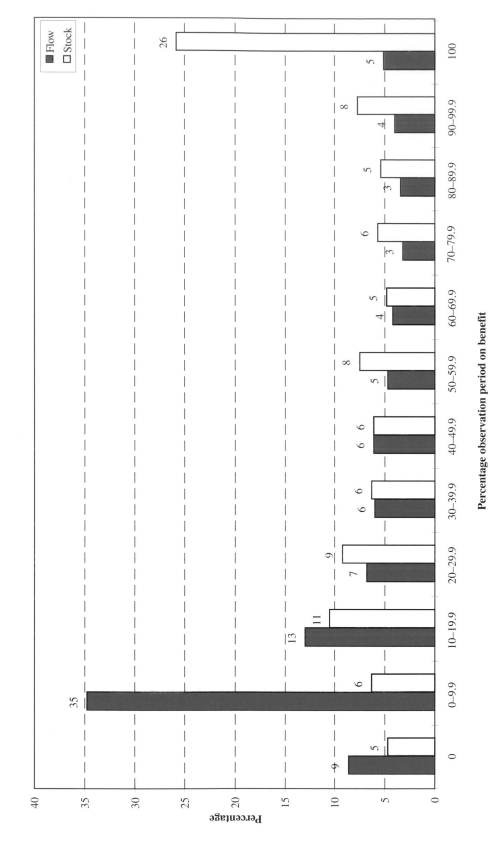

New claimants had spent an average of 30 per cent of time on benefit (standard deviation 32 per cent), although the median value of 14 per cent confirms that there were a few very long durations, and many which were rather short. For the stock of claimants, the mean was 58 per cent (standard deviation 36 per cent), indicating that they have claimed for a greater proportion of the observation period. Indeed one-quarter (26 per cent) of the stock sample had claimed benefit for the whole of the observation period.

In later stages of the data analysis, attention will be focused on the length of time claimants spend on benefit and the factors which contribute to moving off. In order to establish some baselines, benefit spell length will now be discussed briefly. A benefit spell is defined as an uninterrupted benefit claim. Some respondents were claiming benefit at the start of the observation period, and therefore the length of claim prior to this point is added to the observed length for these claimants.

All spells not completed at the end of the observation period are excluded from the following figures as their 'final' length is unknown. Chapter 8 discusses the effect of their exclusion: incomplete spells may be longer than observed completed spells. Table 2.8 displays descriptive statistics of completed benefit spell length for both flow and stock samples. By definition, each respondent also has exactly one incomplete spell – the current spell (2,142 for the flow; 2,685 for the stock). Hence there were more completed than uncompleted spells for the flow, and the similar numbers for the stock, confirming the view that the flow are move likely to change status than the stock.

Table 2.8   Completed benefit spell length (weeks)[5]

Statistic	Flow	Stock
Mean	37.2	64.6
Standard deviation	76.8	105.8
Median	9	26
Maximum	908	1,178
Minimum	1	1
Base (number of spells)	2,331	2,696

The relatively large standard deviations, and differences between means and medians, suggest that there are a few very long durations: not typical of most respondents. If the median is chosen as a less biased estimate, new claimants spent an average of two months claiming benefit. In comparison, the stock spent an average of six months claiming benefit. The figure for the flow is smaller because the data are based upon completed spells and many of the values contributed by the flow (particularly from single spell claimants) will

5   The base is the number of completed spells as some claimants 'contributed' more than
    one completed spell.

be restricted by the time lapse between signing on and off. Both samples contained extreme values; the maximum spell length was 1,178 weeks, more than 22 years.

2.4 Economic activity
2.4.1 Economic activity prior to interview

There was a gap between selection and interview. Consequently, not all who were signing on at the time of selection were doing so at the interview. Table 2.9 shows the main economic activity of new and stock claimants in the week before the interview.

Table 2.9   Economic activity prior to interview[6]

Vocational qualification	Flow		Stock	
	Number	Column per cent	Number	Column per cent
In work/education/training				
Full-time work (30+ hours)	526	22	480	10
Part-time work (16 to 29 hours)	129	5	130	3
Part-time work (less than 16 hours)	58	2	144	3
Full-time education and part-time work	13	1	14	*
Full-time education only	48	2	75	2
Government/TEC/LEC programme	129	5	210	4
Total	903	37	1,053	22
Looking for work				
Unemployed and looking for work	1,446	60	3,486	74
Not looking for work				
Looking after home/children	17	1	40	1
Health problems/disability/injury	41	2	94	2
Pregnant/had baby	2	*	6	*
Retired	2	*	6	*
Abroad/on holiday	6	*	6	*
Caring for adult	3	*	4	*
Total	71	3	156	3
Other	10	*	35	1
Missing	–	–	1	*
Overall total	2,431		4,732	

* = less than 0.5 per cent, more than zero;   – = true zero

Unsurprisingly, the most common activity was unemployment. Almost three-quarters (74 per cent) of the stock of claimants were unemployed and three-fifths (60 per cent) of the flow were still unemployed and looking for work the week before the interview. The difference between these two figures highlights a fundamental contrast between the samples: the new claimants appear to have a better chance of signing off within a relatively

---

6   Each of the categories is mutually exclusive and governed by respondents' *main* activity.

short period of time than do the stock, many of whom are longer term claimants. This is also reflected in the proportion of both samples who were either working or undergoing some form of training. Over 37 per cent of the new claimants were in such an activity in the week prior to interview whereas only 22 per cent of the stock were similarly occupied. Twice as many new claimants as existing claimants managed to obtain full-time work. There was the same type of difference between the two samples for those moving into part-time employment (16 to 29 hours per week).

Around three per cent of new and existing claimants were recorded as not looking for work. For many of these respondents (two per cent of all respondents in both samples), this was due to health problems or a disability, but a number (less than one per cent of all respondents) classed their principal activity as looking after the home or children (or both).

2.4.2 Most recent and usual jobs Eighty-five per cent of the flow and 79 per cent of the stock of respondents had been in paid employment during the three years prior to their last/current spell of claiming benefit. The most frequently cited occupations were: building labourers (two per cent in the flow; four per cent in the stock); sales assistants (four per cent); goods vehicle drivers (two and three per cent); packers (two and three per cent); storekeepers (three and two per cent); cleaners (two and three per cent) and clerks (four and three per cent). Although it is difficult to make assertions on the basis of such small percentages, any occupation with a higher proportion in the stock than the flow may be one in which those working in that field find it more difficult to return to work. Of the jobs noted here, this most clearly applies to building labourers – a clear reflection of labour market trends and the shift from manual to non-manual work in recent years (Machin, 1993, cited in Balls and Gregg, 1993). Chapter 3 builds on this analysis.

About 71 per cent of new and 64 per cent of existing claimants indicated that they thought of themselves as having a 'usual' job or one which they had worked in more than any other. When prompted to nominate this job, the responses closely matched those offered as the most recent job. The most common were: clerks (four per cent of the flow; three per cent of the stock); sales assistants (four and three per cent); building labourers (two and four per cent); goods vehicle drivers (two and three per cent); and managers/proprietors in service industries (two per cent).

2.4.3 Economic activity during the observation period Information about respondents' activities during the two years prior to the interview was collected from the Work Benefit History Sheet, and a number of supplementary questionnaire items. Seven per cent of the flow sample and eight per cent of the stock stated that they had never worked. These claimants tended to be much younger than average (a mean of 21 years for new claimants; 24 years for all claimants), greatly influenced by the recent school leavers present in this group. Table 2.10 shows the percentage of respondents who reported spending at least some time in each of the main economic activities from Table 2.8.

Four-fifths of new claimants had done either full- or part-time work during the two-year observation period, compared to 57 per cent of the stock. Consequently, 43 per cent of the stock had not done any paid work during the previous two years, whereas just 21 per cent of new claimants had not worked in that time. A much larger proportion of new claimants reported being in full-time education during the two-year period. It may be remembered that the timing of the sample will have meant that a disproportionately high number of new claimants will have been college leavers, and this is likely to explain the difference. Relatively few respondents (around three per cent) reported spending any time devoted to a mix of full-time education and part-time work, or to looking after the home or children as their main activity.

Table 2.10 Percentage performing each economic activity during the observation period

Activity[7]	Percentages	
	Flow	Stock
In work/education/training		
Any full- or part-time work	79	57
Full-time work (30+ hours)	70	48
Part-time work (16 to 29 hours)	15	9
Part-time work (less than 16 hours)	7	8
Full-time education and part-time work	6	3
Full-time education only	17	12
Government/TEC/LEC programme	17	7
Looking for work		
Unemployed and looking for work	97	98
Not looking for work		
Looking after home/children	4	4
Health problems/disability/injury	8	7
Other	11	9

Two per cent of the stock and three per cent of the flow had not given their principal activity as 'unemployed and looking for work' at any time during the observation period. It might be expected that all respondents would have described their activity as such at some point. Most of these respondents gave their principal activities as either working part-time for fewer than 16 hours per week or not working for health reasons. These respondents were, of course, still able to claim benefit during the observation period.

---

7 Many respondents had more than one activity during the observation period, so totals sum to rather more than 100 per cent.

2.5 Partners Interviews were also obtained from most partners of the main respondents. Of the 4,876 (unweighted) respondents, 2,035 had live-in partners (42 per cent) and interviews were obtained from 1,495 (a 73 per cent response rate). A description of these partners is given in this section. The data are weighted in the same manner as the main respondents.

Three-quarters (75 per cent) of the partners of flow respondents from whom interviews were secured were female, compared to 85 per cent of stock partners. Female partners (78 per cent of all female partners granting interviews) were more willing to be interviewed than male partners (62 per cent).

Male partners were older on average than female partners, men having a mean of 40 years (flow and stock) and women 37 years in the flow, 38 in the stock. Just over 38 per cent of flow partners and 36 per cent of stock partners stated that they had signed on at some time; 31 per cent and 24 per cent respectively had signed on in the last two years.

Partners were most commonly in full-time work or looking after the home or children (see Table 2.11). Relatively few (eight per cent in both flow and stock samples) were unemployed and looking for work. More of the stock sample were recorded as looking after the home or children than in the flow sample (54 and 36 per cent respectively) due to the greater preponderance of females as partners of stock claimants, and the fact that these roles are more traditionally adopted by women. This also partly explains the difference in the proportion of flow and stock sample partners in full-time work (32 and 18 per cent respectively).

Table 2.11 Economic activity of partners in week prior to interview

Activity	Flow		Stock	
	Number	Column per cent	Number	Column per cent
Full-time work (30+ hours)	208	32	241	18
Part-time work (16 to 29 hours)	66	10	67	5
Part-time work (less than 16 hours)	41	6	72	6
Full-time education and part-time work	4	1	3	*
Full-time education only	7	1	11	1
Government/TEC/LEC programme	2	*	5	*
Unemployed and looking for work	52	8	104	8
Looking after home/children	231	36	709	54
Health problems/disability/injury	27	4	76	6
Pregnant/had baby	2	*	8	1
Retired	5	1	9	1
Abroad/on holiday	1	*	4	*
Other	3	1	3	*
Overall Total	651	100	1,313	100

* = less than 0.5 per cent, more than zero

Claimants with partners may face difficult and complex decisions about employment. A number of work strategies are possible, all of which impact upon benefit entitlement. To give an indication of the types of 'economic activity' among couples, the main and partner respondents were grouped into three categories: in work, education or training, 'unemployed and looking for work', and those not working and not looking for work. Table 2.12 shows the number and percentage of each of the nine combinations (three for each partner) in both flow and stock samples in the week prior to interview.

The single category accounting for most partnerships was where one partner was unemployed and looking for work with the other partner not working and not looking. This was found in 29 per cent of flow partnerships and 49 per cent of stock partnerships, the vast majority of which had the main respondent as the unemployed partner.

In the week prior to interview, 27 per cent of the adults in flow partnerships were both in work, whereas just 11 per cent of stock partnerships were similarly occupied. Around six per cent of the flow and seven per cent of the stock partnerships were both unemployed and looking for work and just one per cent of flow and four per cent of stock respondent–partner pairings classed themselves as not working and not looking for work. Almost a quarter (23 per cent) of flow partnerships and just under a fifth (19 per cent) of stock partnerships had one partner in work or education or in training and the other partner unemployed and looking for work.

Table 2.12   Economic activity of partners in week prior to interview

Respondent activity	Partner activity	Flow		Stock	
		Number	Column per cent	Number	Column per cent
Work, etc.	Work, etc.	172	27	144	11
Work, etc.	Unemployed	11	2	15	1
Work, etc.	Inactive	76	12	119	9
Unemployed	Work, etc.	140	22	239	18
Unemployed	Unemployed	41	6	87	7
Unemployed	Inactive	189	29	645	49
Inactive	Work, etc.	16	3	15	1
Inactive	Unemployed	–	–	2	*
Inactive	Inactive	5	1	46	4
Total		651		1,312	

* = less than 0.5 per cent, more than zero; – = true zero

2.6 Conclusion   This chapter described the respondents to the survey. Comparisons between new and all claimants were made throughout the chapter. Men were found to be over-represented in the stock sample, indicating that they accumulate within the system and thus find it more difficult to sign off. The stock of claimants were also generally older.

Around a half of all claimants either lived alone or with their parents. The former were more prevalent in the sample of all claimants whilst the latter accounted for a higher proportion of the new claimants. Another notable difference between flow and stock samples was the relatively high proportion of non-manual workers in the flow sample. Almost half of the flow sample had held white-collar jobs, compared to two-fifths of the stock sample (excluding those without regular occupations). In itself, this finding suggests that manual workers are likely to remain on benefit longer than non-manual workers (manual workers may also be more likely to become unemployed, but separate evidence from a sample of the employed would be needed to be used to examine this possibility).

Three-quarters of respondents had qualifications of some kind. This demonstrated an increase over comparative figures from eight years before the current survey (Garman, Redmond and Lonsdale, 1992). Newer claimants were slightly more likely to have academic qualifications than the stock. The most common vocational qualification was the City & Guilds Part 1, held by an eighth of all respondents.

On average, the stock of claimants had been signing on for around six months, but this obscured the fact that a number had been signing on for much longer. Income Support was received by around three-quarters of those signing on and Unemployment Benefit by a third. The latter benefit was more common among new signers than longer term claimants.

Since being sampled, 37 per cent of the flow and 22 per cent of the stock had moved on to either a job or some form of education or training scheme. Sixty per cent of the flow and 74 per cent of the stock remained unemployed and looking for work. During the two-year observation period prior to the interview, four-fifths of the flow had worked, in contrast to three-fifths of all claimants.

Seventy-three per cent of all live-in partners participated in the survey, although female partners were more likely to participate than male. The economic activity of these partners were primarily: in work (full-time or part-time); and looking after the home or children. Only one in seventeen households contained main respondents and partners who were both unemployed.

3 THE LABOUR MARKET BACKGROUND OF THE UNEMPLOYED

Overview
Chapter 2 provided a description of unemployed people, focusing on their current circumstances and their labour market activities in the preceding two years. The aim of this chapter is to investigate in more detail people's longer term work experience, built up before their most recent spell of signing on as unemployed.

This chapter will shed light on two particular areas of interest. It will consider how far the unemployed vary by their duration of unemployment, and how far they differ from the employed (since it is possible to compare a number of characteristics of unemployed people with those of people in jobs, using the Labour Force Survey). How far does unemployment affect all social groups, or some more than others? Second, the chapter will examine some aspects of 'human capital': the skills and experiences that may help the unemployed back into work. It will be the Wave 2 data collection that will enable a clearer discussion of this area, and permit analysis of to what extent favourable labour market backgrounds assist movement off Unemployment Benefit and Income Support.

The emphasis is on the previous **work** experience of the unemployed, and this is examined in relation to a variety of personal characteristics, including age and duration of unemployment. The chapter begins with longer term labour market experience (Section 3.1), then looks at respondents' economic activity prior to signing on (Section 3.2), and then at their last job before they became unemployed (Section 3.3).

3.1 Experience of work
There are a number of ways of measuring previous work experience. Chapter 2 has already analysed data from the two or three years prior to the interview, and used quantitative measurements of lengths of spells unemployed, signing on, and so on. This chapter uses a summary indicator of previous labour market experience. Each respondent was provided with a list of possible scenarios, that might have described their prior work experience. These included such descriptions as: '*I have spent most of my life in steady jobs*,' and '*Before now, I've never been unemployed.*' They were then asked to say which — if any — applied to them. This is a more 'subjective' measure than one based on quantitative data, but is easy to interpret and should provide an accurate impression of work experience to date. Table 3.1 provides the full wording of the questions and replies, and shows results for the stock and flow samples within the survey.

The responses from both the stock of unemployed, and more recent claimants, were surprisingly similar. The largest group was those who had spent most of their working life in steady jobs. This accounted for 44 per cent of the inflow sample, and 39 per cent of the stock sample. Equal proportions (seven per cent) said they had never been unemployed before, but a greater proportion of the stock sample said they had spent more time unemployed than in work (16 per cent compared to nine per cent of the flow).

Table 3.1   Previous labour market activity

B.29 Other people have summed up their experience of work in the ways shown on this card. Are any of them things that you would say about yourself?

The table shows which description applies 'the best'.

		Column percentages
	Flow	Stock
I have spent most of my working life in steady jobs	44	39
I've mainly done casual or short-term work	11	10
I've spent a lot of time out of work due to sickness/injury	1	2
I have spent most of my working life self-employed	3	3
Before now, I've never been unemployed	7	7
I've spent more time unemployed than in work	9	16
I have been in work, then out of work, several times over	13	13
I have spent a lot of my adult life looking after the home and family	3	4
None of these apply	9	7
Not stated or missing data	*	*
Unweighted base (= 100%)	2,387	2,440
Weighted Base (= 100%)	2,431	4,482

* = less than 0.5 per cent, more than zero

It is important to understand the pattern of women's labour market participation as well as men's. Previous experience is a factor in this. Women were many times more likely to have spent time looking after the home and family – this was the description that applied best to eight per cent of women in the flow and to 12 per cent of women in the stock – compared to around one per cent of men in both groups. Men were more likely to have worked mostly as self-employed (four per cent of men, compared to one per cent of women, among both the stock of unemployed and the flow), or to have been in and out of work several times over (true for 15 per cent of men, compared to nine per cent of women in the flow and eight per cent of women in the unemployed stock). Women were also twice as likely to say that none of the descriptions applied to them (12 per cent of women compared to six per cent of men), suggesting some gender bias in the categories offered.

The above section showed that the previous labour market experience of men was quite similar to that of women. However there were clear differences in background among unemployed claimants of various ages. Those aged 45 years or more were the most likely to have had 'steady jobs', accounting for around two-thirds of this age group (62 per cent of 45–54-

year-olds; 69 per cent of those aged 55 or more). Younger respondents were quite likely to say that the classification did not apply to them (17 per cent of those aged under 25). They were also most likely have been unemployed for more than they had been employed (26 per cent of the youngest group, and 20 per cent of those aged 25–34), which was very rare among the oldest groups (just two to three per cent of those 45 years or older). Experience of casual or short-term work was also strongly a characteristic of the younger age groups (see Table 3.2), accounting for almost one in five (18 per cent) of those under 25 years of age.

Table 3.2   Previous labour market activity

Age group		Statement			Column percentages	
	Under 25	25–34	35–44	45–54	55 and older	All ages
I have spent most of my working life in steady jobs	17	35	46	62	69	39
I've mainly done casual or short-term work	18	11	6	1	2	10
I've spent a lot of time out of work due to sickness/injury	2	2	2	1	2	2
I have spent most of my working life self-employed	1	3	6	3	4	3
Before now, I've never been unemployed	8	4	5	10	9	7
I've spent more time unemployed than in work	26	20	10	2	3	16
I have been in work, then out of work, several times over	11	17	16	10	6	13
I have spent a lot of my adult life looking after the home and family	1	2	6	8	6	4
None of these apply	17	6	3	1	–	17
Not stated or missing data	–	1	*	1	*	*
Unweighted base (= 100%)	1,375	1,293	952	819	436	4,876
Weighted Base (= 100%)	1,307	1,388	931	723	382	4,732

* = less than 0.5 per cent, more than zero; – = true zero

Labour market experience was strongly linked with the time that people had been unemployed in their current spell. This is shown in Figure 3.1. Unsurprisingly, the longer people had spent unemployed in their current spell, the more likely they were to say they had spent more time unemployed, than employed. Indeed, approaching one in three of the longer term unemployed described themselves in this way (31 per cent of those unemployed four to five years; 29 per cent of those unemployed at least five years).

The longer term unemployed were also more likely to have been in and out of work several times over (25 per cent of those unemployed for five or more years). Among those continuously unemployed for at least the last four years, a relatively low proportion said they had mostly worked in steady jobs (26 per cent, compared to 39 per cent of all stock cases), and only quite a low proportion had mostly done casual or short-term work (two per cent, compared to ten per cent of all stock cases) when they were in paid work.

There is an important debate about whether the long-term unemployed are somehow different from those who have shorter spells at the outset of their claim, or whether it is the experience of being long-term unemployed that makes them appear different. From a policy point of view, could those likely to be long-term unemployed be identified by their characteristics at signing on, rather than by 'watching' them become long-term unemployed? This question has no easy answer, and would require separate detailed examination. However, as Figure 3.1 indicates, it is possible that previous labour market experience would provide some discrimination between those likely to be unemployed longer term, and those more likely to move out of unemployment. The counter-argument is that the question used will give different answers as a result of unemployment itself. Those unemployed for the longest periods would, almost by definition, emphasise the time they had spent unemployed. Fuller longitudinal information would be needed to track such a possibility.

Figure 3.1   Previous labour market experience by length of current spell of unemployment

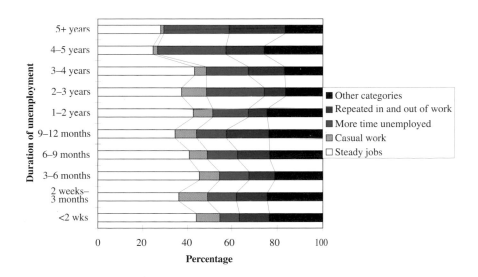

3.2 Economic activity before current spell of claiming

The previous section used a summary measure of work experience, taken over the whole (working) life-course. An alternative approach is to look at economic activity just prior to the current spell of signing on as unemployed. A summary breakdown of activity prior to signing on is shown in Table 3.3. The most common prior activity was being in work, true for 60 per cent of the sample. A total of 18 per cent had been either on a training programme, or in full-time education. The remaining 23 per cent of respondents were in a range of roles prior to signing on, including being unemployed (but not signing on), looking after the home, or recovering from health problems.

Table 3.3   Economic activity prior to signing on as unemployed

Activity before signing	Column percentages
In work	60
On a training programme	10
In full-time education	8
Other/inactive	23
Missing/not stated	*
Weighted total (= 100%)	4,732

* = less than 0.5 per cent, more than zero

The next sections compare and contrast the characteristics of the unemployed, by their previous employment status.

3.2.1 Age   The group who had just left full-time education were, unsurprisingly, usually younger than those in the other groups. In fact, 61 per cent of those who were in full-time education before signing on were younger than 25 years old (compared to 28 per cent of the total stock of unemployed).

Those leaving education tended to be single. Only 11 per cent of those entering unemployment from full-time education had a partner, compared to 37 per cent overall, and as many as 42 per cent of those who were working prior to signing on. Those formerly on training courses, before moving on to unemployment-related benefits, also tended to be younger than average: those in work just prior to unemployment were the oldest.

3.2.2 Children   Younger respondents, those older than 45, and those without current partners, are less likely to have children of dependent age. As few as seven per cent of those entering unemployment from full-time education had any dependent children, compared to 30 per cent in the sample as a whole, and 35 per cent of those previously working.

3.2.3 Sex   Men outnumbered women by almost three to one in the stock of unemployed (74 per cent are male): see Figure 2.1 in Chapter 2. For those previously in work, or on training programmes, this ratio increases to three-and-a-half to one: 78 per cent of those working just prior to claiming were men, as were 77 per cent of those finishing a training programme. Among those coming from full-time education, or from other routes, the figure is much lower at two to one: 65 per cent of those completing education were men, as were 67 per cent of those from other routes.

3.2.4 Ethnic group   The overwhelming majority (89 per cent) of the sample were of white ethnic status. As many as 91 per cent of those working just prior to claiming were white: but higher proportions of non-white groups were not working prior to signing on. A total of 23 per cent of those leaving full-time education were not white: including five per cent who said they were Indian, three per cent who said they were Pakistani, and four per cent who gave 'other' replies. Among those coming from training programmes, 90 per cent described themselves as white; there was a lower than average proportion of whites among those from 'other' backgrounds (86 per cent) – also see Table 2.4 in Chapter 2.

3.3 Previous jobs   A number of studies have suggested strong links between unemployment and the changing industrial and occupational profile of employment. White (1991) and Gregg (1993) argued that unemployment was largely the result of the 'shake-out' of full-time, relatively well-paid manual jobs in the manufacturing and construction sectors. People – usually men – losing such jobs were confronted by vacancies which were often part-time, in services, with lower pay, and often seen as more likely to be taken by women. It is usually argued that the major change that led to higher unemployment is a reduction in the likelihood of such people finding jobs once unemployed, rather than any greatly increased risk of them losing the job in the first place.

The previous section looked at economic activity prior to signing on as unemployed. The majority (60 per cent) had come from a paid job, but a sizeable minority had come from other situations. The focus of this next section is on respondents' last job. Questions about a person's last job were asked whether or not they were in work just prior to signing on, so this section includes those who might have left training or education prior to signing on.[1] Whilst information about a person's 'usual' job was also collected, more detailed and more consistent information is available for the last job, and hence this latter concept is the focus of discussion. Comparisons are made with the employed population, as represented in the Labour Force Survey.

3.3.1 Occupation   Table 3.4 compares the previous occupations of the unemployed, with the distribution of current occupations of those in employment.

There are some clear differences between the occupations of the employed, and the previous occupations of the unemployed. The employed population is much more likely to be in professional or managerial occupations. More than one in three (35 per cent) of those in employment could be described as being in managerial or professional occupations (Standard Occupational

---

1 Not all respondents were asked about their last job. This question was asked of those:
   • who were working in the week before signing on
   • who had any paid job since October 1993
   • who had worked at some time in the three years prior to signing on, even if prior to October 1993.

Classification (SOC) groups 1–3), compared with 18 per cent of those recently unemployed (the flow) and 17 per cent of those in the stock of unemployed. The unemployed were also more likely to have come from a 'craft' background, or have been plant/machine operators.

Table 3.4   Last occupation of unemployed compared to occupations of those in employment

Last or current occupation: SOC major group	All in employment: LFS Sep–Nov 1995	Unemployed – flow	Unemployed – stock
Managers and administrators	16	8	9
Professional occupations	10	5	3
Associate professional and technical	9	5	5
Clerical and secretarial	15	16	11
Craft and related	13	16	18
Personal and protective services	11	13	11
Selling	8	8	6
Plant and machine operators	10	14	16
Other occupations[2]	8	15	21
Unweighted Total (= 100%)	n/a	1,980	1,988

Source for all in employment: *Labour Force Survey Quarterly Bulletin*, No. 15, March 1996.

In fact these comparisons may *understate* just how different the unemployed are from those of the population in employment. The figures for those in employment include both full-time and part-time work, where the latter is less likely to be high status, whereas most of the unemployed are male former full-time workers. A comparison solely with full-time workers would, however, tend to *overstate* such differences. The figures for the unemployed also exclude a small group those who have not held a job for some time, whose previous job might be expected to be of a lower occupational standing.

3.3.2 Industry   This section now compares the industries of those in employment with the former industries of the unemployed. This information is available only for the last job held. As with occupation, there are clear differences between the industrial profiles of the employed and the formerly employed, though of a lesser degree than might have been expected. The unemployed were more likely to have worked in the construction sector, accounting for 12 per cent of the last jobs of the unemployed flow and 16 per cent of the unemployed stock, than were the employed population at the same point in time, amongst whom just seven per cent were in the construction sector. The unemployed were less likely to be working either in public administration or 'banking and finance', than are the employed population. Almost a

---

2 'Other occupations' comprises a range of jobs not described by the preceding categories. The largest groups within this range were 'building labourers', 'cleaners and domestic', 'kitchen hands' and 'other labourers'.

quarter (24 per cent) of those employed work in public administration. This compares with only around one in seven (13 per cent) of the unemployed who used to work in this industry. Moreover, 'banking and finance' accounts for 14 per cent of employment, but rather less than ten per cent of the prior industries of the unemployed (nine per cent of the flow and seven per cent of the stock).

Table 3.5   Last industry of unemployed compared to industry of those in employment

Last industry SIC major group	All in employment: LFS Sep–Nov 1995	Unemployed – flow	Unemployed – stock
Agriculture	2	3	2
Energy	1	3	2
Manufacturing	19	22	23
Construction	7	12	16
Distribution	20	24	23
Transport	6	7	7
Banking	14	9	7
Public administration	24	15	13
Other services	6	6	6
Unweighted sample (= 100%)	n/a	1,980	1,988

Source for all in employment: *Labour Force Survey Quarterly Bulletin,* No. 15, March 1996.

3.3.3 Responsibilities   Most of the sample had not had managerial or supervisory duties in their previous job. Eleven per cent said they had had managerial responsibilities (slightly higher for men); the same proportion said they had had supervisory authority (slightly higher for women). Thus 78 per cent had had neither set of duties. Those who had been unemployed for longer than four years were less likely to have had either set of responsibilities, but otherwise there appeared to be no link between duration of unemployment spell and whether a respondent used to have these types of duty.

3.3.4 Employment status   In their previous job, 86 per cent were employees, 11 per cent were self-employed, and a residual two per cent either did not say or did not know.[3] Women were much less likely than men to have been self-employed: only three per cent of women used to be self-employed compared to 14 per cent of men. Self-employment was most common for those aged between 35 and 44 years of age (17 per cent), and those aged 45 to 54 (13 per cent), but was unusual among the young unemployed (seven per cent of those younger than 25 years).

The self-employed were typically sole traders or subcontractors. In 86 per cent of cases they had no paid employees. Thirteen per cent of the self-

3   This is a non-trivial level of non-response. It may be worth pointing out that different definitions of self-employment are used between tax law, social security law and employment law – which could lead to uncertainty.

employed had had businesses employing 1–24 paid employees and barely one per cent had had 25 or more employees.

3.3.5 Hours of work   The sample was selected not because they were unemployed, but through claiming as unemployed. A successful claim for Unemployment Benefit requires sufficient previous work experience to have established enough of a National Insurance Contributions record. For Income Support, a claim requires that any partner is working fewer than 16 hours each week. Therefore we might expect previous jobs to have been principally of a full-time, 'breadwinner' status, and indeed this turns out to the case (see Figure 3.2).

The hours worked by employees tended to cluster around 40 hours per week, especially among men. There was a clear peak at around 40 hours per week. A sizeable number of men worked longer hours; for women there was a significant group working shorter hours. Whilst one-quarter of women in this study worked fewer than 24 hours a week in their previous job, the bottom quarter of men were working up to 37 hours a week. One-quarter of men had worked 50 or more hours each week in their previous job. Men had worked an average of 45.2 hours in their previous job, compared to 34.7 hours for women. These are rather longer working weeks for men than found among even full-time employees – in Autumn 1995 full-time employed men were working an average of 40.9 hours a week – but are more typical for full-time employed women who had an average working week of 34.8 hours (*Labour Force Survey Quarterly Bulletin,* No. 15).

Figure 3.2   Employees' hours of work in last job before current spell of unemployment

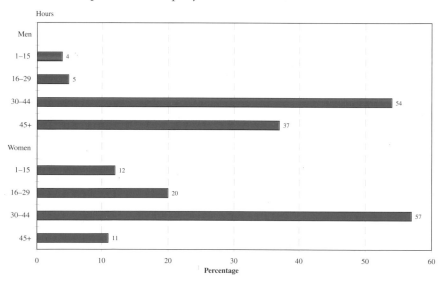

Those formerly self-employed worked longer hours than employees. The self-employed worked for an average of 55.3 hours, compared to 42.4 hours

among employees, although this includes quite a few very long and very short working weeks among the self-employed.

3.3.6 Pay level   Respondents previously employed were asked for their (exact) former earnings, whilst those leaving self-employment were asked to estimate their income within fixed bands (e.g. £100–49, £150–99, etc.). Among employees, there were a small number of very high former earnings quoted. These types of figures can tend to dominate any descriptive measures so, in the following sections, the top one per cent (each claiming to have earned more than £1,000 per week) have simply been dropped when calculating the average. A measure much less affected by a few high extreme values is the 'median', defined as the level at which half earn more, and half earn less, for any given group. This measure will also be used to make sensible comparisons.

The average earnings of those whose last job was as an employee were £158 per week, with a median figure of £138. Earnings tended to be higher for men (average £172, compared to £118 for women). And, as shown in Figure 3.3, earnings also tended to vary with the age of the unemployed person. For men, previous earnings peaked for those aged 45–54 years. This seems consistent with a 'life-cycle' view of earnings, where earnings rise as a reward to greater experience (Mincer, 1974). For women, earnings were at their highest for those aged 35–44 years although – with an average around £135 in this age range – female earnings were well below those of men.

Figure 3.3   Average earnings in last job before unemployment spell

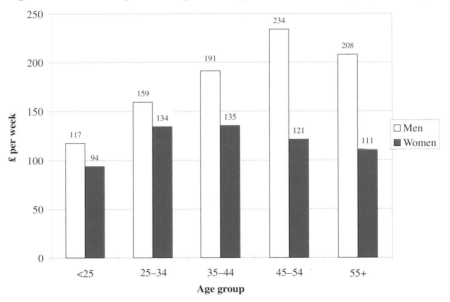

To some extent, of course, the earnings differences between men and women in their prior jobs reflect differences in hours worked. Men are likely to have been working longer hours than women, and there was a clear relationship between previous hours and level of earnings. Compared to the overall average of £158 per week, those who used to work 45 hours a week (or longer) had average earnings of £212 (with a median figure of £180). It is predominantly men working such lengthy hours.

Table 3.6   Previous earnings level of the self-employed

Weekly income	Column per cent
Under £50	7
£50–99	8
£100–49	12
£150–99	13
£200–49	13
£250–99	10
£300–99	15
£400–99	7
£500–99	2
£600 or more	1
Other	1
Can't say	6
Not answered/refused	5
Base (= 100%)	429

The incomes of the self-employed are notoriously difficult to measure, for a mix of practical and conceptual reasons (Boden and Corden, 1994). In this study a simple expedient – trying to identify income within certain boundaries – was adopted and the results appear in Table 3.6. As might be expected there were a few quite low levels of income, some 'bunching' towards the centre, and a few higher values. The median level of income was in the range £200–49. On the surface, this seems considerably higher than that reported by employees. This may reflect differences in knowledge, and in how respondents have treated expenses that may be deducted from tax liabilities. It may also reflect the fact that the self-employed tended to be older, and were more likely to be male, both factors associated with higher levels of earnings among the former employees in this study.

3.3.7 Reasons for leaving last job This section examines why the previous job ended, which may be important for several reasons. It may be important in assessing benefit eligibility, since leaving a job without 'good cause' may lead to a benefit suspension (of up to 26 weeks). Those being made redundant may have benefited from a lump-sum payment, and therefore have entered unemployment with greater financial resources than those leaving at the end of a fixed term contract. In fact, respondents' last jobs ended for a large number of reasons, the most common:

- being 'made redundant' (23 per cent)

- that a temporary job had come to an end (16 per cent)

- that the person resigned or decided to leave (16 per cent)

- that a fixed term contract had ended (11 per cent)

• that the company had gone out of business (nine per cent).

Men were slightly more likely than women to have been made redundant (24 per cent compared to 21 per cent), and more likely to have left a job because their company went out of business (11 per cent of men compared to six per cent of women). Women were more likely to have 'decided to leave' (19 per cent of women, but 15 per cent of men), or to have cited family/personal reasons for leaving work (11 per cent of women compared to three per cent of men).

The longer a person had been unemployed, generally the more likely they were to have left their previous job through being made redundant. Redundancy accounted for 32 per cent of those unemployed more than five years, and 26 per cent of those unemployed for 3–5 years, compared to 23 per cent overall. There were also clear patterns by age (see Figure 3.4). The younger respondents were more likely to have left a temporary or fixed term job, to have resigned voluntarily, or to have cited health problems as a reason to leave. Older respondents were the most likely to have been made redundant. Those between 35 and 44 years of age were the most likely to have left a job when their company stopped trading.

Figure 3.4   Reasons for leaving last job, by age at interview

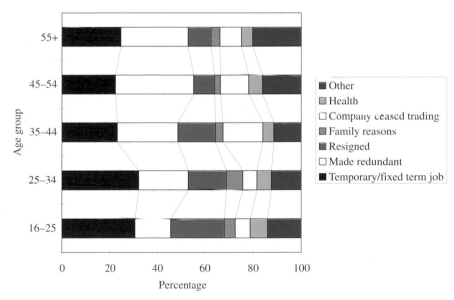

3.3.8 *Education courses*   A proportion of the sample (367 cases, weighted, or eight per cent) was in full-time education prior to signing on. They were more likely to have been studying for academic rather than vocational qualifications. The fact that the sample was drawn during the summer months may have led to an over-representation of students in the sample, as Appendix A points out. Almost three in ten (29 per cent) had been studying for a degree, the most common course, and a further five per cent had been studying for 'A' levels. On the more vocational side, one in ten had been on an HNC/HND course, three per cent had been working towards on ONC/OND, and six per cent were taking a Business and Technology Education Council (BTEC) course. NVQs (and Scottish equivalents) were mentioned by a further three per cent of respondents, and nine per cent mentioned one of a mixed range of other vocational qualifications. A large proportion (one in five of this group) provided answers too vague to be confident about identification, or seemed unable to be clear about what they had been studying.

3.4 Conclusions

This chapter has examined the labour market patterns of unemployed claimants prior to their most recent spell of signing on. The emphasis has been on any forms of work undertaken. This provides an important background against which to assess observed movements off benefit in the future.

By and large, there are clear differences between the occupations and industries of the employed population, compared to the former status of the claimant unemployed. The unemployed are less likely to have worked in professional and managerial occupations, and more likely to have left a job in manufacturing or construction. But these differences should not be exaggerated. The unemployed are a diverse group, with significant numbers having a professional or managerial type of background. A small proportion were previously on very high salaries, but these were very much the minority.

There were a number of differences between the longer and shorter term unemployed. This provide some hints about which groups are likely to remain unemployed for longer, and hence remain in the stock. With a single survey, however, it is not readily possible to separate the effects of longer duration, from those of age, or other related characteristics. Again, analysis of data collected subsequently will be illuminating.

Overview A central objective of Jobseeker's Allowance and its associated changes is to make clearer the conditions and obligations inherent in benefit receipt (see Chapter 1). Jobseeker's Allowance develops the pre-existing structure of conditionality and built on Unemployment Benefit/Income Support procedures. This chapter discusses some of the main rules concerning unemployment-related benefits. It investigates claimants' understanding of the responsibilities and obligations inherent in the previous system, focusing on the main conditions of benefit receipt. It also looks at their understanding, and experience, of various sanctions that can be imposed on claimants.

The first section of the chapter (4.1) is devoted to a consideration of respondents' knowledge of the rules governing 'signing on', 'making a claim' and the meaning of being available for, and actively seeking, work. The second section (4.2) explores claimants' understanding of the possible reasons for being disallowed or disqualified from benefit while the third (4.3) discusses the extent and experience of disqualification and disallowance.

4.1 Understanding 'signing on', 'availability' and 'actively seeking work' A central objective of Jobseeker's Allowance and its associated changes is to make clearer the conditions and obligations inherent in benefit receipt (see Chapter 1). Perhaps the key new instrument is the Jobseeker's Agreement. This is a document that has to be signed by both the claimant and the Employment Service for benefit to be received. The officers cannot sign an agreement unless, based on its content, they are convinced the claimant will satisfy the requirements of being available for, and actively seeking, work (Poynter and Martin, 1996). The Jobseeker's Agreement represents a new instrument, not just an development of the older Back to Work Plan. The Jobseeker's Agreement is compulsory, whereas the Back to Work Plan was voluntary. It may specify other conditions on which benefit entitlement depends – also a new feature – although the key labour market conditions (of being available for and actively seeking work) apply rather than of following the Agreement to the letter.

This procedure is supported by other changes intended to create a clearer, more consistent benefit structure and improved service delivery. Physically locating the Benefits Agency component of Jobseeker's Allowance within Employment Service Jobcentres reduces the need for customers to visit different offices and also emphasises the link between the receipt of benefit, and the obligation to engage in effective job-search. Moreover, the Labour Market System computer system, which provides an instant record of each claimant's history of job-search activity and of former and current agreements, enables Employment Service staff actively to monitor claimants and provide assistance every time they sign on.

The scheme is therefore expected to bring about changes in people's perception of the contract inherent in benefit receipt, in their appreciation of the obligation to look for work and in the diligence and effectiveness of their job-search. It is also expected to increase claimants' understanding of the benefit regime, both in work and when unemployed, and of the financial benefits of employment.

Most of these developments refine and make more explicit the pre-existing structure of conditionality and build on Unemployment Benefit/Income Support procedures. Therefore, in providing a foundation for monitoring the impact of Jobseeker's Allowance it was necessary first, in this chapter, to investigate claimants' understanding of the responsibilities and obligations inherent in the Unemployment Benefit/Income Support system and secondly, in Chapter 5, to consider their experience of administrative procedures.

Unemployment Benefit, and Income Support for persons unemployed, was conditional on a person 'signing on' at pre-determined intervals (usually each fortnight) and their being 'available for work', and 'actively seeking work'. People who do not satisfy either of the latter two conditions are generally *disallowed* unemployment-related benefits. In addition benefit can be withheld (or reduced) in circumstances where a claimant takes, or fails to take, some action and in doing so unreasonably causes or perpetuates their unemployment and as a result is *disqualified*. Examples of where disqualification might apply include leaving a job without *just cause* or failing, without *good cause*, to take up a job or a place on a training course.

This chapter describes respondents' understanding of the rules covering the conditionality of benefit, and about disallowance and disqualification. However, the rules are quite complex and a lengthy structured questionnaire is not necessarily the way to explore the depths of people's knowledge. Consequently, complementary qualitative research by Cragg Ross Dawson on Claimants and the Benefit System, and Centre for Research in Social Policy on Disallowance and Disqualification, seek to uncover the reasoning behind the statistical findings. Nevertheless, the current findings are in themselves important as they reveal a lack of clarity and detail in claimants' understanding of the (then) current rules relating to unemployment related benefits.

4.1.1 Signing on Signing on is a condition of benefit payment, and usually claimants must 'sign on' by visiting the Jobcentre each fortnight, typically on a weekday. On occasion, people may be required to sign on more frequently (even daily). This would usually indicate some concern about whether the claimant was engaged in fraud (such as working while signing). Although procedures vary from office to office, claimants are generally given a half-hour period during which they are expected to sign on. The transaction itself takes a matter of minutes but, in the last couple of years, staff have been increasingly encouraged to engage customers in 'active signing'. This means asking clients about their job-search and any successes since last signing. Staff are briefed to offer basic advice or information, and to refer on to specialist advisers as appropriate (see Chapter 5).

Under the system of Unemployment Benefit and Income Support, unemployed claimants who lived more than six miles from a Jobcentre (or Unemployment Benefit Office), were generally allowed to sign on by post. Under Jobseeker's Allowance, the rule is based on one hour's travelling time either way, unless the claimant would have to be away from home for more than four hours in total.

Towards the end of the research interview, after a section in which respondents explained how they went about searching for work, respondents were reminded of the start of their current or last spell of unemployment and presented with a very general question about signing on:

- *As you may know, there are some rules about signing on as unemployed. Which of these rules have you heard about?*

The aim of the question was to elicit which, if any, rules relating to signing on were particularly salient. Interviewers were briefed to probe thoroughly, but not to prompt. In coding the replies, 21 different responses were distinguished: the average respondent offered 2.6 separate rules. For the most part, respondents trawled all the rules that they could recall governing the receipt of unemployment-related benefits. Relatively few were able spontaneously to focus on the rules relating to signing on. However, as we shall see later (Chapter 5), a third (32 per cent) of respondents recognised that they had to sign on in order that their benefit be paid.

While respondents mentioned a large number of rules and conditions, comparatively few noted the same ones; indeed only three were recalled by more than one-sixth of the sample: the need to be actively seeking work, to be available for work and to report a return to work.

a) Reporting obligations
The set of 'rules' that appeared to have most salience were the obligation to report things affecting benefit eligibility (Figure 4.1a). Thirty per cent mentioned the requirement to sign off benefit as soon as a job was secured and 18 per cent noted that it was necessary to declare work done while on benefit. These people, at least, were aware of the uniquely important role that employment plays in access to social assistance in Britain and, hence, the need to notify the authorities of developments in this area. Far fewer claimants (three per cent) spontaneously mentioned the need to report other changes in circumstances, an issue recently considered in relation to (general) Income Support (Sainsbury, Hutton and Ditch, 1996).

Figure 4.1   Knowledge of rules about signing on

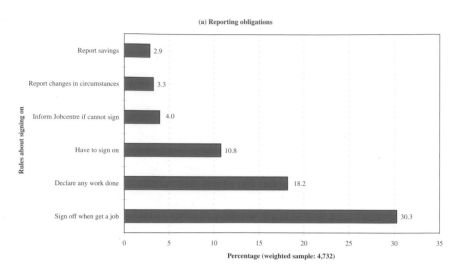

Only 11 per cent volunteered the fact you have to sign on, some noting that to do so was a condition of benefit receipt. Another four per cent mentioned the need to inform the Jobcentre if, for whatever reason, they were unable to attend when required. It is possible that others simply took it for granted that you had to sign on.

b) Labour market obligations/conditionality

The second set of responses reveal some understanding of claimants' obligations to look for work (Figure 4.1b). Thirty per cent cited the requirement to seek work, 15 per cent the need to be available for work, and two per cent the obligation to accept a job if it were offered. Of particular importance, given the centrality of the Jobseeker's Agreement under the changed benefit regime, is the very small number of respondents (fewer than one per cent) who mentioned Back to Work Plans. In fact, Back to Work Plans were voluntary, unlike the new Jobseeeker's Agreement which is a condition of benefit receipt. About 71 per cent of recent claimants (defined, here, as respondents applying within 12 weeks of the research interview) could remember agreeing a plan at the start of their claim, but for most people it is clearly not at the front of their mind or seen to be linked to the process of signing on.

Figure 4.1   Knowledge of rules about signing on

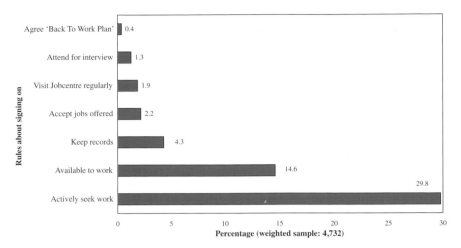

(b) Labour market obligations

Small numbers of people also mentioned the need to visit the Jobcentre regularly, to attend if called to a Restart[1] interview (not surprisingly more often mentioned by long-term claimants) and four per cent referred to the need to keep records of the actions that they had taken to find work. Given that 52 per cent of respondents did, in fact, keep notes on their job-search activity, this last finding is less disturbing than at first sight. Records play a more important role under Jobseeker's Allowance now that claimants are obliged to follow the terms of their Jobseeker's Agreement.

c) Formal requirements
There were some people who noted aspects of the conditionality of benefit receipt (Figure 4.1c). Seven per cent said that you had to be made redundant in order to receive benefit. Again without qualitative work it is impossible to assess how literally this was meant, and whether it embraced more or less than the notion of leaving a job without just cause. Smaller numbers noted that older workers did not have to sign on, and that signing depended on marital status although we cannot be sure what respondents had in mind – perhaps the need for just one adult in a couple to sign on for Income Support purposes.

---

1   People who have been unemployed for six months are usually invited to attend a
    Restart interview at which a range of options are discussed; see Chapter 5 for more
    details.

Figure 4.1 Knowledge of rules about signing on

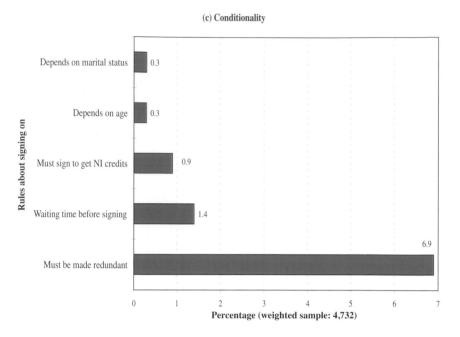

(c) Conditionality

d) Restrictions

For completeness, it is necessary to mention the comparatively few people who reported the constraint on the amount of time that claimants are allowed to work or study while signing on (Figure 4.1d). Rather more recent claimants than long-term recipients drew attention to these rules. We cannot say whether this was because they were more likely to remember it from their meeting with the New Claims Adviser, or because the rules were a more salient constraint on behaviour, or for some other reason.

Figure 4.1   Knowledge of rules about signing on

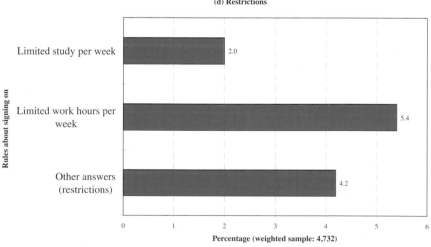

(d) Restrictions

One might have expected some differences in claimants' understanding of the rules about signing on, perhaps varying according to the benefit they were claiming and the length of time they had been claiming it, their history of unemployment, age or family circumstances. In fact, there was no strong evidence of such relationships, and few exceptions to this generalisation. It is possible that new claimants (five per cent) were less likely than other people, especially those who had already moved off benefit by the time of the survey interview (11 per cent), to mention the need to have been made redundant. Those with a history of sickness (11 per cent) were also perhaps more likely than those without (four per cent) to stress the need to keep records. Otherwise, people responded to the question on signing on in very much the same way.

It would appear, therefore, that however much respondents had signed on and regardless of the circumstances, their understanding of the basic rationale for doing so remained unaltered. They recognised the obligation to report major changes in circumstances, notably finding a job, but little importance was attached to the conditionality of benefit receipt and few respondents seemed to have a detailed appreciation of the rules about signing, certainly at a conceptual level. Indeed, 13 per cent could not recall any rules at all including two per cent of respondents who said that nobody had ever told them about any rules. The length of time a person had been claiming did not seem to affect their ability to remember rules, although the level of their education apparently did so. Fifteen per cent of respondents without paper qualifications could not spontaneously recall any rules relating to signing on compared with eight per cent of those with qualifications. Even so, this latter figure is considerable given the importance of signing on as an instrument of policy.

4.1.2 Actively seeking work   We have seen that about one in three respondents associated signing on with the requirement actively to be seeking work.[2] But what did respondents understand by the concept of actively looking for work? The new Jobseeker's Allowance Regulations talk of taking reasonable steps to find a job. Welfare rights workers have noted that while *'taking a single step during a week to find a job will not be enough unless taking that step on that occasion was all that was reasonable'* the 'implication *is that taking two steps a week will be enough* generally' (Poynter and Martin, 1996, page 21 – our emphasis). The Jobseeker's Allowance Regulations further amplify the concept of 'step' to include making written or oral applications, seeking information, registering with an agency and appointing someone else to help find work. However taking two steps may not be enough in itself: it is for Adjudication Officers to determine whether the steps taken were reasonable, taking into account a jobseeker's individual circumstances.

However, very little understanding of this detail was elicited in response to the survey question, which took the form:

---

2   Indeed, as we shall see later (Chapter 5), a large majority of claimants believed that the main reason why they had to sign on was to give the Employment Service a means of checking that they were indeed seeking work.

- *A further requirement for signing on as unemployed is that the person must be 'actively seeking work'. What do you understand 'actively seeking work' to mean?*

Again, more insight will come from qualitative research. Nevertheless it may reasonably be deduced that most unemployed claimants have generally not thought much beyond the common sense meaning of the phrase 'actively seeking work'.

A large number of respondents did little more than substitute simpler words (Figure 4.2). Twenty-seven per cent translated the concept as 'to look for work' while almost twice as many, 52 per cent, introduced the notion of vacancies in place of work. Some respondents were a little more specific about how one might be expected actively to look for work. One-fifth said applying for jobs and attending interviews, and two per cent mentioned Job Clubs.

Figure 4.2   Knowing about 'actively seeking work'

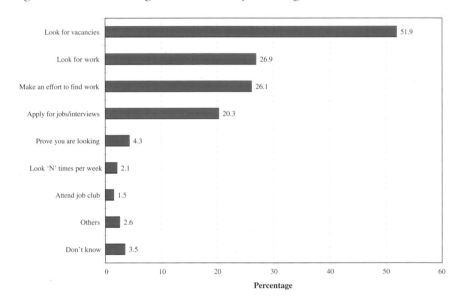

To a sizeable minority of respondents the behavioural requirements of the term 'actively' were clear. Twenty-six per cent talked of 'making an effort' to find work, perhaps with the implication that one not only had to look for work but also to demonstrate to somebody else that one was looking. On the other hand, very few referred to the need to keep records in order to prove that one had been actively seeking work. Only two per cent mentioned a need to look for work on a particular number of occasions each week.

There is some evidence that respondents differed in the language that they used when talking about the concept of actively seeking work. Those without qualifications were somewhat more likely to use the phrase 'look for work' rather than 'look for vacancies' than was the case amongst respondents with qualifications (Figure 4.3). The latter were more likely to talk about 'making an effort to find work' than were those without qualifications.

Respondents who described their work experience as 'mostly self-employed' were somewhat more likely than most (32 per cent as against 27 per cent) to say that the obligation was 'to look for work', perhaps interpreted in the sense of continuing with promoting their business, and less likely to talk of 'applying for jobs' (12 per cent did so compared with 21 per cent of other respondents).

Figure 4.3   Actively seeking work: terminology and educational qualifications

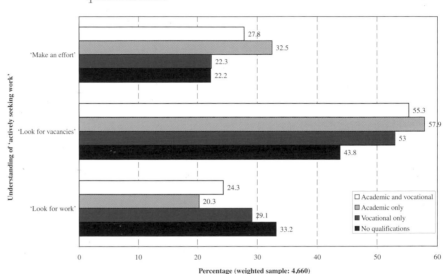

Generally, though, respondents differed little in the meaning that they attached to the notion of actively seeking work. Moreover, while acknowledging that surveys have limits for exploring what people understand by certain concepts, there was little evidence that unemployed claimants either always bracket benefit receipt together with the obligation to seek work, or dwell on the need to demonstrate that they are seeking work in order to receive benefit. Judging by the evidence presented elsewhere in this report (Chapter 7), most respondents were looking for work to get a job. The fact that the rules require as much was a lesser consideration in people's actions.

4.1.3 Availability for work
To claim unemployment-related benefits a person has to be capable of work, that is neither ill nor disabled, and available for work as an employed earner. Availability is not just a matter of time, although a claimant is usually expected to be available to work immediately; it also applies to the nature of employment.

As a general rule, claimants with recent work or training experience are allowed to restrict their availability to their 'normal occupation' for a maximum of the first 13 weeks on benefit (the 'permitted period'). Thereafter they are not allowed to impose restrictions on for example, the type or location of work, working conditions or wages unless they can prove that they still have a reasonable chance of obtaining a job or that the restrictions are consistent with their physical or mental condition. While refusing an offer of self-employment is not taken to affect availability, only being available for self-employment after a 'permitted period' does not count as being available under the terms of the legislation.

Presented with an open question on availability of the same form as before, the most frequently mentioned aspect was that which related to time, namely, being able to start work, and 48 per cent recognised that this generally meant straight away (Figure 4.4).

Whereas, in this case, a majority of claimants were able to give an account approximating to the conditions for benefit receipt, only a minority mentioned the other side of availability. A fifth (21 per cent) said that they had to be prepared to accept any job. Hardly anyone distinguished the specific conditions sufficiently clearly for them to be separately coded. Just six per cent noted that their availability could not generally be affected by other commitments.

Figure 4.4   Knowing about 'availability for work'

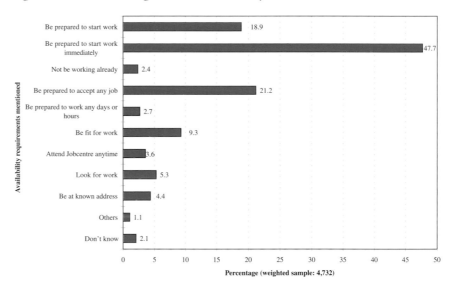

Most of the other points that respondents raised linked with the concept of actively seeking work (in the interview introduced after availability). One exception was fitness for work, mentioned by nine per cent of respondents (including 28 per cent of those with a history of health problems); another was the requirement to be contactable at home other than for two weeks in every year which was cited by four per cent of respondents.

As with the other conditions of benefit receipt, there was remarkably little difference in understanding between different types of claimant. Respondents who had already left benefit by the time of interview were a little less likely to remember the requirement to be able to start work immediately (45 per cent compared to 49 per cent). Also, this same point did seem to be mentioned with increasing frequency as the length of a person's spell on benefit rose from between one and three months (42 per cent) to between one and two years (54 per cent). However, the proportion of people on benefit for less than a month who recalled this condition for benefit receipt (49 per cent) was not discernible from that of claimants of two or more years (48 per cent).

It would appear, then, that most claimants' understanding of the conditions and obligations inherent in the receipt of unemployment benefit is rudimentary. It is worth acknowledging, however, that it is difficult to address many of these issues during a long interview covering a range of different types of **mostly factual** information. Qualitative research in already commissioned work currently in the field should clarify this. Perhaps, given time more prompting and more astute questions, respondents would have been able to recount the rules in greater detail. What we can say is that there little evidence that the implicit contract between the state providing benefit, and the claimant being ready to take and actively to seek work, was uppermost in claimants' minds. Ninety-four per cent of respondents already felt that it was their 'responsibility to look for a job', although as many as ten per cent agreed that they 'wouldn't bother looking for a job if benefit did not depend on it' (see Chapter 6).

4.2 Understanding disallowance and disqualification

As noted above, persons who fail to meet the conditions of being available for employment or actively seeking it are *disallowed* from benefit. Should they change their labour market behaviour, other things discounted, they instantly become eligible for benefit. People who satisfy the basic conditions of entitlement but who through omission and commission unreasonably become or remain unemployed and are thereby *disqualified* and have their benefit reduced or denied for up to 26 weeks.[3] During this period there is, in effect, nothing that a person can do to have their entitlement to benefit instated or reinstated. People who are disallowed receive no Unemployment Benefit or Income Support (except possibly the latter at a reduced rate on hardship grounds), whereas someone who is disqualified receives Income Support but at a reduced rate (his/her entitlement to up to 12 months' Unemployment Benefit generally being set aside until the end of the period of disqualification).

The main grounds for disqualification include:

• dismissal for misconduct

• voluntarily leaving a job or giving up a place on a training scheme

• failure to apply for a job or training course notified by the Jobcentre

• failure to take up any other opportunity of employment

---

3 This figure primarily applies to voluntary unemployment. Different rules apply to cases of industrial action, being abroad or being imprisoned.

- refusal to accept a job or training place that is offered

- failure to attend a Restart interview

- failure to carry out written recommendations provided by the Employment Service

- unemployment resulting from a trade dispute.

The decision to disqualify a person is taken by an Adjudication Officer on the grounds that the person did not have good or just cause for the action that he/she took, and the decision and the period of disqualification are generally open to appeal. While disqualification and disallowance are conceptually distinct, distinctions can be quite murky in practice. A person who refuses to take up employment without good cause may be treated as 'unavailable for work' and disallowed Unemployment Benefit for up to six months. While such a job remains open there is also no entitlement to Income Support, except under hardship provisions. When the vacancy is filled, entitlement to Income Support may be re-established, though at a lower rate so that the effect of the Unemployment Benefit disqualification is not nullified.

The question exploring claimants' understanding of these rules was in the section covering respondents' dealings with the Employment Service. It followed questions about any directions that had been given to them by Jobcentre staff. Respondents were first asked:

- *Do you know that in some circumstances unemployed persons can have their benefit stopped or reduced?*

Eighty-four per cent did know this.

Respondents were then separately asked 'the reasons that benefit can be stopped' and 'the reasons it can be reduced'. Perhaps unwisely the question did not distinguish between Income Support and Unemployment Benefit though respondents are often unaware of the differences between benefit rules. Replies are presented in Figures 4.5a and b – these are codes grouped from the open-ended questions.

Figure 4.5a   Stopping benefit

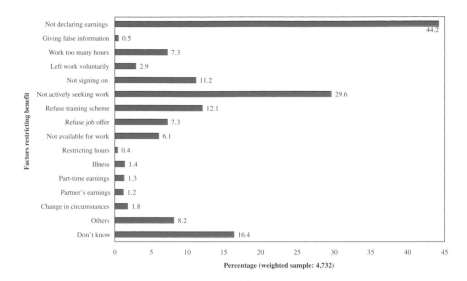

Given the complexity of the regulations, it is not surprising that there is considerable degree of confusion among respondents as to their meaning. Forty-four per cent of all respondents (including those who did not know that benefit could be stopped) replied to the question in terms of benefit being terminated because earnings were not declared; that is on grounds of fraud rather than non-compliance. Similarly five per cent mentioned the stopping of benefit as a result of giving false information.

Another nine per cent referred to people working too many hours, and some of these respondents may also have had fraud in mind if they meant that the hours had not been declared. Alternatively, they may simply have been noting the fact that Income Support is payable only to people working less than 16 hours per week, in which case they were interpreting the question in terms of basic eligibility criteria rather than sanctions. (Similar numbers believed that benefit could be restricted for working too many hours (eight per cent) or for not declaring earnings (six per cent) which is not generally the case.) A confusion with basic eligibility is similarly revealed by the 17 per cent of respondents who cited part-time earnings as a reason for reducing benefit.

Figure 4.5b   Restricting benefit

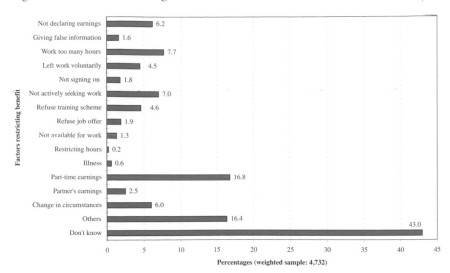

Percentages (weighted sample: 4,732)

Whereas, in this case, a majority of claimants were able to give an account approximating to the conditions for benefit receipt, only a minority mentioned the other side of availability. A fifth (21 per cent) said that they had to be prepared to accept any job. Hardly anyone distinguished the specific conditions sufficiently clearly for them to be separately coded. Just six per cent noted that their availability could not generally be affected by other commitments.

The fact that so few respondents thought to mention becoming voluntarily unemployed may accurately reflect the low salience, or limited awareness, of this as a trigger for sanctions. Certainly this view is supported by the evidence presented below (Section 4.3). However, attention should be drawn to the placing of the question immediately after those concerned with directives given by Jobcentre staff. This may have set reactions to these directives as the respondents' frame of reference in answering about disallowances and disqualifications.

There were a handful of differences between groups of respondents in the priority given to the various reasons for benefit being stopped or restricted.[4] Most evident was the salience of the consequences of refusing to attend an Employment Service programme among those whose spell on benefit had lasted more than 12 months: almost 27 per cent of long-term unemployed mentioned these compared with just seven per cent of other claimants. (Referral to Employment Service Programmes, under mandatory attendance rules which can affect benefit, generally begins at 12 months' unemployment, although Training following Restart interviews would start after six months.) For less understandable reasons the long-term unemployed were slightly less likely to mention the failure to declare work as a reason for

---

4   All the percentages given in this and the subsequent paragraph relate to the base of people knowing that benefit could be stopped under certain circumstances.

benefit being stopped (46 per cent compared to 54 per cent of other respondents).

The pattern of responses of respondents who were receiving only Unemployment Benefit also differed very slightly from those of other respondents, although all the differences are small and not all readily explicable. They were more likely to cite lack of availability for work and working too many hours, and less likely to mention not signing or attending for interview and refusing to attend an Employment Service scheme (Figure 4.6). Finally, it is perhaps worth noting that the youngest respondents, those aged under 25, were very slightly more likely to mention leaving a job as a reason for stopping benefit than older respondents (seven per cent as against three per cent).

Figure 4.6   Stopping benefit and benefit received

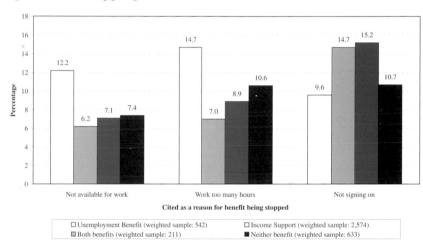

Again then, to summarise, we find only a limited appreciation of the obligations inherent in benefit receipt and the likely consequences of breaching them. There was almost certainly a confusion in some people's minds between eligibility for benefit and sanctions, a confusion which may have been exacerbated by the form of the questions asked, though other approaches would also have weaknesses. Equally, though, there was no strong evidence that many people could confidently negotiate their way around the concepts and regulations in this area.

4.3 The experience of disallowance and disqualification

4.3.1 Reduced benefits

So far in this chapter we have reported on respondents' understanding of the rules and obligations associated with the receipt of unemployment-related benefits. In this section we briefly discuss the characteristics of people who reported being disallowed or disqualified from benefit for labour market reasons. The information relates only to the circumstances relating to the start of claimants' current award, or for respondents who had already moved off benefit, their most recent claim. As a consequence, it does not take account of the experiences of people who may have been disqualified or disallowed subsequently or during earlier claims.

First, it is important to recognise that people can receive less than the maximum amount of benefit for a number of reasons. The question asked of respondents was:

- '... did you get the full amount of benefit as a result of your initial claim, or not?'

This allowed the respondent to determine what the full amount of benefit might have been and, therefore, some will have deduced that they were initially paid less than the 'full amount' only on account of their benefit subsequently rising. Moreover, a few respondents might even have mistakenly taken an increase in benefit arising from an uprating as evidence that they had been disallowed or disqualified. As a consequence the extent of disallowances or disqualification among respondents might be overstated.

Altogether a quarter of people reported initially receiving less than the full amount of benefit, with the largest group of these (61 per cent) being paid a reduced level of benefit for a period of time (Table 4.1). Given claimants' limited understanding of the regulations, which is emerging as a main theme in this chapter, it is perhaps to be expected that the majority of the applicants who did not receive full benefit were taken by surprise. With the exception of people who received only National Insurance credits, only around a third of respondents knew that they would not get a full award, a fraction that fell to one-quarter (26 per cent) for the comparatively small group who received no benefit whatsoever.

4.3.2 Disqualification and disallowance

Only a minority of those who failed to be awarded what they believed to be full benefit were disallowed or disqualified (Figure 4.7). Not all respondents knew why they had not received full benefit and, in fact, 30 per cent claimed that nobody, either from the Employment Service or the Benefits Agency, had explained to them why this was so. This is despite everyone being formally notified for the reasons. Some respondents gave a series of reasons and account is taken of all of these in the results in Figure 4.7[5]. Overall, between 30 per cent and 40 per cent might have had benefit stopped or reduced for labour market reasons although another quarter of respondents presented either one of a large range of explanations or none.

---

5   There was hardly any difference in the distribution of first and subsequent answers. A possible exception was the withholding of an award while a person's circumstances were investigated; this was mentioned by seven per cent of people as the first reason but by ten per cent overall.

Table 4.1 Respondents receiving and not receiving 'full amount of benefit'

Type of benefit 'loss'	Expectation of loss of benefit			All 'losing' benefit	Those 'losing' benefit	All
	Yes	No	Other (mainly don't know)	Number	Per cent	Per cent
Reduced benefit for duration	35	63	2	725	61	15
Refused benefit for duration	33	65	2	196	16	4
Refused benefit altogether	26	69	5	84	7	4
NI credits only	55	41	4	188	16	2
Full benefit	–	–	–	–	–	72
Others (including missing information)	–	–	–	–	–	3
Base					1,192	4,732

Figure 4.7 Reported reason why benefit was stopped or restricted

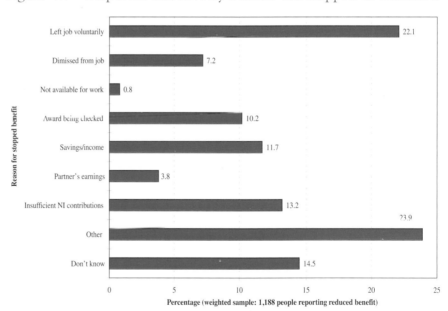

Percentage (weighted sample: 1,188 people reporting reduced benefit)

The majority of those who appear to have been either disqualified or disallowed, some 22 per cent of the respondents who did not receive full benefit, seemingly left a job voluntarily and another seven per cent were dismissed. Apparently very small numbers lost benefit through not being available for work and only three people in the entire (unweighted) sample were disallowed on the grounds that they would only accept a specific kind of job. Finally, it is appropriate to draw attention to people who reported receiving a reduced benefit while the factual details of their claim were being checked. This seems to have been the experience of one in ten of all respondents claiming not to have received full benefit, but it was more often introduced as a supplementary factor than were other reasons (Figure 4.7).

Not everybody who reported leaving their job voluntarily or being dismissed lost benefit, nor did all those who believed that they had been disqualified for these reasons cite them as the triggers for leaving their last job (Table 4.2). Some 23 per cent of respondents left their last job voluntarily or were dismissed, of whom 51 per cent said that they initially received less than full benefit. People leaving work for 'family reasons' were less likely to report losing benefit, but those who were dismissed were no more or less likely to lose benefit than those who resigned for other than family reasons. Sometimes the reasons given for being disallowed appeared inconsistent with the circumstances of leaving work, suggesting a lack of understanding of the rules. There are no clear reasons why those who gave 'family reasons' should have been sanctioned, but this may reflect a difference between stated reasons for leaving a job and the official interpretation. Only one-third (36 per cent) of the 62 respondents who were dismissed and had their benefit reduced or stopped cited the dismissal as contributing to the loss of benefit. Half (51 per cent) who left for other than family reasons said that their choice to leave work had meant the loss of benefit.

Table 4.2   Reasons for sanction and leaving last job

| | | | Column percentages | |
| Reported reason for 'sanction' | Reason given for leaving last job | | | |
	Resigned	Family reasons	Dismissed[6]	All three
'Sanctioned' for reason given for leaving	28	14	20	23
'Sanctioned' for other reason	27	16	35	27
Not sanctioned	45	70	46	49
Base	578	165	316	1,059

Although only a small proportion (between seven and ten per cent) of new claimants in the survey lost some or all of their benefit for labour market reasons, when grossed up to national figures, the number of people affected is large. Official figures indicate that, in 1995/6, 237,500 people were disallowed benefit (Unemployment Benefit or Income Support for unemployment) on the grounds of their not being available or actively seeking work, or for refusing employment; this is respectively 46 per cent and 360 per cent more than in 1994/5 and 1992/3. It is worth noting, too, that the increased numbers of disqualifications and disallowances in recent years are not clearly reflected in the stock sample of respondents (Figure 4.8). Had one found such a pattern it would have suggested that claimants sanctioned left benefit at the same rate as those who received full benefit. The fact that this pattern is not evident points to the possibility that claimants

---

6 Includes people dismissed for committing an offence.

who are sanctioned tend to remain on benefit (Unemployment Benefit and/or Income Support) for longer than other claimants, although not too much weight should be placed on this observation.

Figure 4.8   Disallowances and disqualifications by date of claim

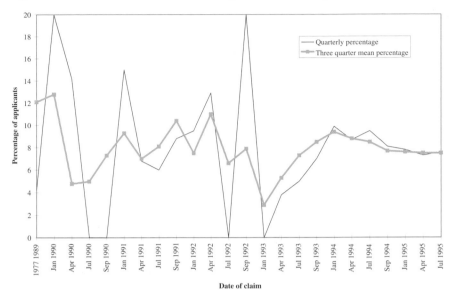

4.3.3 Claimants disallowed or disqualified

People of all socio-demographic groups appeared to have had their benefit reduced or stopped because of voluntary unemployment. That said, respondents with certain characteristics were notably more prevalent among the group who reported receiving less than full benefit on account of their leaving a job voluntarily or being dismissed (Figure 4.9). The most striking associations were with age and occupation. Forty-two per cent of people losing work for these reasons were aged under 25 (26 per cent under 21) compared with 28 per cent and 13 per cent of all respondents. Only 25 people (in the unweighted sample) had their benefit affected on account of their not being available for work but 13 of these were aged less than 25.

Age and family type are closely related so it is no surprise to find disproportionate numbers of single people disqualified or disallowed. Thirty-one per cent of those affected were single (compared with 24 per cent of the sample as a whole) although it appears that respondents living at home with parents or relatives were no more likely to have had their benefit stopped or reduced. Disproportionate numbers of those dismissed or who left their jobs were manual workers, and most of these had few or no skills.

It is worth noting, however, some of the factors unrelated to the probability of losing benefit on the grounds of voluntary unemployment. Education did not appear to be a predictor nor were personal assessments of job history. Marginally more of the claimants sanctioned described themselves as 'white' but because of the small number of respondents from minority communities this finding was not statistically significant.

Figure 4.9   Characteristics of persons disqualified for voluntary unemployment

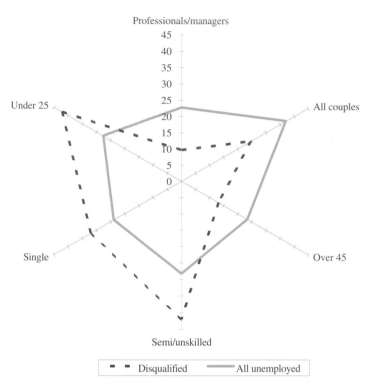

People who were disallowed and disqualified benefit for labour market reasons differed in the extent to which they anticipated sanctions. Half (51 per cent) of those who left their last job of their own accord expected to lose benefit (Table 4.3), of whom 18 per cent reported losing all their benefit for a period of time and 74 per cent some of it. On the other hand, 48 per cent of respondents leaving a job were taken by surprise when their benefit was affected, as were 63 per cent of those that were dismissed. Eighteen out of the 25 people in the unweighted sample (72 per cent) who were disallowed on account of their not being available for work did not expect to lose benefit although in fact 16 (64 per cent) received no benefit at all at least for a period.

Table 4.3   Expectations of reduced or nil benefit

				Row percentages
	Expected reduced or nil benefit			Base
	Yes	No	Other	
Left job voluntarily	51	48	1	263
Dismissed	33	63	4	86
(Not available for work[7]	29	64	7	25)
All receiving reduced or nil benefit	37	61	2	1,188

7 Unweighted figures are used because of the small sample which also means the percentages are subject to a large margin of error. Three respondents are included who said that they placed restrictions on the kind of work that they would do; all three did not expect to lose benefit but did.

The planned changes to disqualifications and disallowances under Jobseeker's Allowance will emphasise the deterrent effect of sanctions. It is not, of course, possible from a sample of claimants to ascertain whether existing procedures were sufficient to deter people from leaving work without good cause. However, the subset of those who said either that they had resigned from their last job, or left for personal reasons, and who subsequently lost some or all of their benefit were asked whether they would still have left their job had they been sure that they would not have received full benefit. In response, only ten per cent said that they would have remained in post, 76 per cent would still have left, while the remaining 14 per cent were, to some extent, unsure. It is clear therefore that the majority of people sanctioned for voluntary unemployment under the existing regime would repeat their actions were they to encounter similar circumstances in future. Under Jobseeker's Allowance, however, the right to automatic hardship payments is removed, and respondents may have been unaware of this change when asked to consider 'similar circumstances' occurring in the future.

4.4 Conclusion   This chapter has focused on claimants' understanding of conditionality in the receipt of unemployment related benefits, prior to the introduction of Jobseeker's Allowance. While it is not easy to probe respondents' detailed knowledge of social security rules and regulations in a structured survey interview, we can be fairly confident about their general level of understanding.

The vast majority of respondents did not spontaneously refer in great detail to the conditionality inherent in receiving unemployment related benefits. People recognised the need to sign on, but very few stated that it was a condition of receiving benefit. Greatest emphasis was given to reporting changes in employment status, finding a job, and therefore the need to sign off as unemployed.

Similarly people may have known that one is required actively to seek work in order to receive benefit, but again any such linkage was rarely mentioned. Most responses amounted to little more than recasting the term 'actively seeking work' into simpler language; even so, only one in four chose spontaneously to translate 'actively' in to anything akin to 'making an effort'. Looking for work was probably best understood as simply that, not as a condition of benefit receipt.

Being available for work meant 'immediately' in the minds of at least half the respondents, and a third noted that they were not allowed to restrict the work that they would accept. Very few people offered any more considered or detailed understanding of the concept of 'available for work'.

Any widespread notion of a contract between claimant and the state was also missing in responses to the questions alluding to disallowance and disqualification. Over half of respondents focused on stopping or reducing benefit as a response to not declaring earnings, fraud or abuse, but far fewer interpreted these powers as sanctions against non-compliance or voluntary unemployment.

This apparent lack of detailed knowledge of the regulations and the concept of conditionality, was general across the entire sample. On the other hand, the seven per cent of respondents who had been disallowed or disqualified tended to be younger, often single and low skilled. That said, 33 per cent of the people sanctioned had none of these characteristics. A common feature among those who were sanctioned, no doubt reflecting widespread ignorance of the rules and regulations, was surprise when they had had benefit stopped or reduced.

A lack of knowledge of the principles underlying benefit receipt does not necessarily imply that claimants would reject them (Table 4.4). Ninety-four per cent of respondents believed that it was their responsibility to find a job, and 73 per cent believed that benefit should be conditional on people proving that they were doing all that they could to get a job. However, respondents were less clear that people should lose benefit if they chose to leave work: 40 per cent thought that they should, and 37 per cent disagreed. (Thirty-one per cent of those who had had benefit deducted because of leaving work voluntarily still agreed with the principle.)

Table 4.4   Attitudes towards the conditionality of benefit

						Row percentages (weighted sample)	
Attitude	Agree strongly	Agree	Neither agree nor disagree	Disagree	Disagree strongly	Other	Base
Personal responsibility[8]	75.3	18.9	3.3	1.3	0.7	0.4	4,683
Actively seeking[9]	41.9	31.0	12.6	8.0	6.2	0.4	4,683
Actively seeking, personal motivation[10]	5.2	4.7	22.6	18.1	48.6	0.9	4,683
Available for work[11]	17.7	29.1	15.6	19.5	17.7	0.4	4,683
Involuntary unemployment[12]	19.6	20.5	22.0	19.4	17.7	0.6	4,638

8   It is my responsibility to look for a job (q1d)

9   Getting benefit should depend on proving you are doing all you can to get a job (q1b)

10 I would not bother looking for a job if my benefit did not depend on it (q2k)

11 Unemployed people should be prepared to take any job they can do and not just a job in their usual occupation (q1e)

12 If somebody chooses to give up their job they should not get their benefit straight away (q1g)

These attitudes, expressed by people who themselves were, or recently had been, unemployed, suggest a bedrock of support for the broad principle of conditionality that is to be made explicit in Jobseeker's Allowance. The findings raise a question about the best method of conveying the message of conditionality under Jobseeker's Allowance, given the level of understanding of obligations and responsibilities under the previous system. Other research suggests claimants prefer clear, straightforward explanations and find the complexity of regulations a hindrance rather than a help (Walker, 1995). People faced with the trauma of unemployment and coping on a low income may well consider that they have more important things to do than explore the labyrinths of social security law (Dobson et al., 1994; Kempson, 1996). Perhaps most people consider conditionality to be irrelevant to them. Certainly this is consistent with the findings presented in Table 4.4 which show that respondents believed that they, personally, did not need to be pressured by the system to look for work. The vast majority of respondents saw it as their responsibility to find work and, when unemployed, most energetically pursued this goal (Chapter 6), probably in the hope of rediscovering the advantages that flow from employment rather than to meet the conditions of receiving benefit.

5 DEALINGS WITH THE EMPLOYMENT SERVICE AND THE BENEFITS AGENCY

Overview One of the objectives of Jobseeker's Allowance is to harmonise the administrative systems of the Benefits Agency and the Employment Service. It is hoped that this will reduce the need for unemployed customers to contact different offices. It should also offer opportunities for improved security and control of abuse (Employment Department/Department of Social Security, 1994).

This chapter describes respondents' reports of their dealings with the Employment Service and Benefits Agency, paying particular attention to those experiences which are thought likely to change following the introduction of Jobseeker's Allowance.

Section 5.1 examines the process of making an initial claim and the number of contacts involved. Section 5.2 considers the fortnightly signing on procedure and evidence of the extent of 'active signing'. Finally, Section 5.3 reports on respondents' experience of interviews with Client Advisers.

5.1 Making a claim for benefit Unemployment Benefit was administered by the Employment Service on behalf of the Department of Social Security while Income Support for unemployed people was the responsibility of the Benefits Agency. Unless living in a rural area, unemployed applicants for either benefit have had to visit a Jobcentre (formerly an Unemployment Benefit Office) to make their first claim and usually attend every fortnight thereafter.

On the first occasion, applicants are usually seen by a new claims receptionist who provides application forms and arranges an interview with a New Claims Adviser, normally on a different day. The Claimant Adviser takes the application forms and discusses an applicant's availability for work based on information supplied by the applicant (on an ES461 form). He/she generally issues a Back to Work Plan, containing steps that the applicant is advised to take. Decisions about availability for work are the responsibility of Adjudication Officers within the Employment Service.

Applications for Income Support are made to the Benefits Agency (on form B1). This is typically issued by the Jobcentre but needs to be mailed or taken to a Benefits Agency office. A Benefits Agency Adjudication Officer decides the outcome of an Income Support claim, but decisions about availability for work are almost invariably based on judgements made by Employment Service staff.

As already noted (Chapter 4), the content of the fortnightly signing on 'interview' has varied over time and differs between offices and officers. In the past it was often a simple formal registration. Now, under the 'active signing' procedures, staff were encouraged to use the Back to Work Plan to structure a brief discussion on the customers' job-search, to offer informed advice, take notes and to refer on to Client Advisers as necessary. Staff are helped by the introduction of the Labour Market System into Jobcentres in undertaking 'active signing'.

Back to Work Plans were reviewed after 13 weeks. Up to two-thirds of claimants may then have to be interviewed, following completion of a UB671JSS. This short interview (15 minutes) checked adherence to the rules, and may have offered assistance with job-search. Thereafter, someone unemployed for six months is invited to attend a Restart interview. They are asked to complete a UB671R form which repeats some questions from the initial claim, but which also asks about job-search and any assistance the claimant would like to help return to work. A range of options is normally discussed and offers of assistance made, perhaps to join a Job Club, Restart course or Training for Work scheme. Failure to attend a Restart interview (twice) can lead to disqualification of benefit. Refusal to take up offers of assistance means that the case is usually passed to an Adjudication Officer to judge whether the person is both available for and actively seeking work.

With the introduction of Jobseeker's Allowance, Benefits Agency staff work alongside Employment Service staff in the same building (usually a Jobcentre). The Back to Work Plan has been superseded by the Jobseeker's Agreement which has to be agreed and signed as a condition of benefit payment. 'Active signing' is likely to be a key element in monitoring adherence to the Jobseeker's Agreement.

Respondents making a new claim within the 12 weeks prior to interview were asked a series of questions covering their recollections of the claiming process. Their responses to these questions provide the subject matter of this section.

5.1.1 Contacts A long-standing complaint sometimes made by some claimants, and which has been repeated in group discussions conducted as recently as Summer 1995 (Stafford et al., 1996), is the need to make repeated visits, and between offices, to make a benefit claim. This is despite the theoretical position in which unemployed applicants are expected to make just two calls at the Jobcentre, first to collect application forms and arrange for an interview with the New Claims Adviser and second to attend for interview. Claims for Income Support can then be made by post. This should remove the need to visit the Benefits Agency, unless further information is required or things fail to run smoothly.

The most common number of visits made by respondents to all organisations before they succeeded in receiving benefit (or National Insurance credits) was indeed two. However nearly as many recalled only a single visit; indeed, 70 per cent of respondents required two or fewer trips successfully to receive benefit (Figure 5.1).[1] The sizeable number of claimants needing only a single visit may cause some surprise. It is probable that a considerable proportion will have telephoned to arrange their new claims interview, completing the necessary forms after arriving at the office. Some may simply have forgotten their initial visit since it may only have taken a short time to fix the interview and may have been combined with another trip. On the other hand, many respondents may have needed to make a special journey, perhaps by public transport, which may impose a limit of the number who just forgot their initial contact with the Employment Service.

Figure 5.1 Visits to make a claim

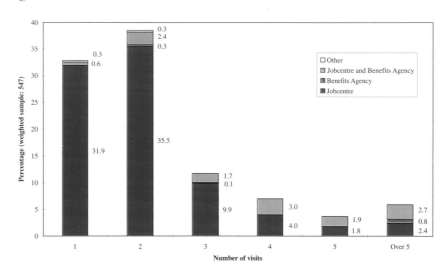

If most people made two or fewer visits, a few made a very large number. Six per cent made at least five visits: the maximum was 40 although this answer sounds like an exaggeration. Most people (82 per cent) needed to visit just one agency only and contact with two agencies was only common among respondents making many contacts. So, even among claimants reporting three visits, four-fifths involved personal contact with a single agency, almost invariably the Employment Service. Indeed, only respondents making more than three visits (fewer than one claimant in six of this group, so figures are based on less than one hundred cases) included a significant proportion (43 per cent) needing to visit the Benefits Agency as well as the Employment Service. Nine per cent of the respondents who visited only a Jobcentre said that they needed to do so on four or more occasions before they obtained their first benefit payment or National Insurance credit.

---

1   Interviewers did not ask eight per cent of the relevant group which offices they visited for reasons which remain inexplicable.

Figure 5.2 Proportion saying that they spent a lot of time going between offices before receiving benefit

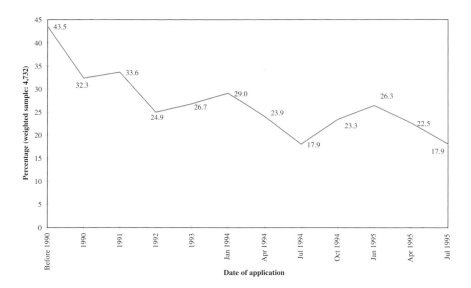

This survey evidence therefore suggests that the problem of customers having to make several visits to and from offices to obtain benefit, which Jobseeker's Allowance is intended to address, is relatively infrequent. Indeed, responses to an evaluative question asked of everybody in the survey, not just those who had had recently applied for benefit, suggest a long-term decline in this practice. The proportion of respondents who answered 'yes' to the question:

- *When you were making your claim did you spend a* lot *of time having to go from one office to another?*:

fell progressively from 44 per cent among people claiming benefit before 1990 to 18 per cent in the third quarter of 1995. However, it should be remembered that long-term recipients will have had a considerable time during which they would have dealt with the two organisations and it may be this experience which colours their responses.

While the number of claimants making several trips to different agencies before receiving benefit may be low, the third or so of respondents who made more than the optimum number of one or two visits represents significant administrative costs, and inconvenience for the individuals concerned. It was not possible in the survey to investigate why some people needed to make more visits than others,[2] but the evidence suggests that respondents with particular characteristics were somewhat more likely than others to make many visits (Figure 5.3 and Table 5.1).

---

2 Related work is about to be published (Stafford et al., 1996a) and more has been commissioned (CRSP, 1996)

Figure 5.3 Visits to claim benefit

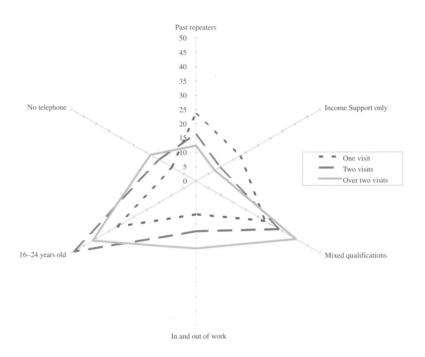

Respondents without telephones (14 per cent of the sample) were at a disadvantage. They were less likely to get their business completed with a single visit (22 per cent did so compared with 35 per cent of those who were on the telephone). Apparently as a direct consequence, 23 per cent had to make a final third visit compared with ten per cent of those with access to a telephone.

The combination of benefits that a person claimed also influenced the number of separate visits made, but the differences were perhaps not as great as expected. Nearly half (47 per cent) the respondents claiming Unemployment Benefit by itself needed to make only a single visit, with a fifth making more than two. The small number of people who claimed a combination of Income Support and Unemployment Benefit appear to have fared worst: 36 per cent made more than two trips but, of these, only two out of seven reported making more than three separate visits.

The number of visits did not seem to depend on claimants' past experience of benefits although respondents who had already left benefit by the time of interview were more likely to require only a single visit and less likely to need many. On the other hand, respondents' own assessments of their careers did reveal a number of groups with unique patterns of experience. Almost one in five of those who said that they had never before been unemployed (18 per cent) made at least six trips to either the Benefits Agency or Jobcentre before getting benefit: a proportion three times the average (six per cent). Moreover, these first time claimants did seem to split

Table 5.1 Visits Made to Claim Benefit

	Number of visits required to receive benefit			Row percentages Base
	1	2	3+	
Benefit status				
Unemployment Benefit	47	33	20	61
Income Support	30	42	28	185
*(Both benefits	26	38	37	20)
Neither benefit	32	37	31	281
Benefit history				
a) Still on benefit				
New claimant	29	38	34	135
Repeat claimant	31	38	30	262
b) No longer on benefit				
New claimant	30	43	27	57
Repeat claimant	43	36	21	97
Work history				
Mostly unemployed	17	50	33	486
In and out of work	22	39	40	95
Never unemployed before	38	29	33	48
*(Mostly self-employed	48	24	28	21)
Possesses telephone				
Yes	35	38	28	469
No	22	40	37	78
Qualifications				
None	35	30	35	107
Vocational	36	41	24	85
Academic	37	41	22	164
Both	26	40	34	185
Age group				
Under 25	25	46	29	225
25–34	34	28	38	141
*(55+	46	25	29	22)
Total	33	38	29	547

* Small base, so percentages have a large margin of error.

quite markedly into those who got their business completed in one or two visits (67 per cent), and those who needed to make a lot of visits, with comparatively few people (15 per cent) falling in between. Unfortunately, the sample is too small to further distinguish the characteristics of these two groups.

Disproportionate numbers of those respondents who characterised themselves as being in and out of work took more than the expected two visits (40 per cent compared with an overall value of 29 per cent). Although, in this case, people clustered around either three (18 per cent) or four or five (16 per cent) visits with perhaps only one in 20 making any more. Claimants who said that they 'had spent more time unemployed than employed' were half as likely as most people to make a single call (only 17 per cent did) although two visits sufficed for another half (50 per cent). Having extensive experience of unemployment therefore does not seem radically to reduce the number of calls required to claim benefit. Possibly respondents are not benefiting from their experience or find that additional visits help them to progress a claim. Perhaps the haphazard nature of their employment history adds to the complexity of their claim.

Perhaps a little surprisingly, claimants who had spent most of their lives as self-employed made fewer visits than any other group. Indeed almost half made a single trip to the Jobcentre (48 per cent). However, since the number of previously self-employed persons in the sample is very small and the pattern does not hold for the unweighted sample, this last finding needs to be treated with caution.

Education also made a difference, though not socio-economic group, but the pattern of the relationship was not very clear. In essence, applicants with both academic and vocational qualifications or without either were more likely than average to make more than the optimal two visits. (Thirty-four per cent and 35 per cent respectively did so, compared with 22 per cent of respondents with other qualifications.) Those with a mixture of academic and vocational training more frequently made a single visit but that was not the case for respondents who left education without acquiring qualifications. What explains this pattern, whether it is linked to age, or perhaps to past employment, is unknown.

Certainly, there does appear to be a quite complex association with age. Respondents younger than 25 were least likely to have made a single visit (only a quarter did so compared with more than a third in other age groups), while those aged between 25 and 34 seemed more often than most to make three or four calls (29 per cent compared with a total sample value of 19 per cent). Finally, while only four per cent of recent claimants were aged 55 or older, they constitute 12 per cent of the group that made six or more calls to get their benefit sorted out.

To summarise, even before the introduction of Jobseeker's Allowance, only small numbers of unemployed respondents have to make large numbers of trips between offices in order successfully to claim benefit. Indeed, access to a telephone means that a third of applicants need only to make one visit in order to sign on and receive benefit. Those making more than two trips include disproportionate numbers of first time claimants, people without telephones, and the older unemployed. Respondents receiving both Income Support and Unemployment Benefit (which will be merged in Jobseeker's Allowance) were few in number constituting four per cent of the sub-sample of recent applicants. Nevertheless, they appear to need to make many visits before receiving their first payment, and therefore have the most to gain from locating both benefits in one office.

5.1.2 New claims interviews

As noted above, a key stage in making a claim for unemployment-related benefit is the new claims interview. Seventy per cent of respondents claiming in the 12 weeks prior to the survey could remember this interview, and they were asked about its purpose, content and value. It is worth pointing out that those previously on benefit, perhaps off benefit only a short time, or those with immediate prospects of work or training, usually have a much shorter New Claims Interview. The breakdown of the remaining 30 per cent shows that 18 per cent said they definitely did *not* have a new claims interview and five per cent were unsure. Unfortunately interviewer errors mean a little over seven per cent of respondents who should have been asked this question were not.

Of those asked the relevant question, three-quarters could remember their new claims interview and one-quarter could not. The proportion who *did* remember the new claims interview was highest among the older respondents – as many as 85 per cent of those aged 55 or older. The proportion of those remembering this interview was also higher than average among those with a recent previous spell of claiming ('repeat' claimants, looking back over the past two years) – it was 74 per cent for this group, compared with 79 per cent among current claimants who not had not been previously unemployed claimants in the two years before the interview.

The new claims interview has a number of objectives. Using information from the ES461 form, the New Claims Adviser establishes whether the applicant is available for work, and the extent to which they are actively seeking work. If these points are in doubt the case will be referred to an Adjudication Officer, a process which may account for some of the ten per cent of cases who reported not initially receiving full benefit while further investigations were conducted (Chapter 4). The Adviser will also discuss approaches to seeking work, discuss vacancies that the applicant may already have seen and get the jobseeker to agree a Back to Work Plan. Advisers are also expected to take a claim for Unemployment Benefit and to advise on Income Support applications.

These different components were familiar to respondents, although individual claimants rarely spontaneously mentioned them all in response to the open question:

• *What do you think was the purpose of the interview with the Adviser when you made your claim?*

After providing a list of reasons – 60 per cent provided more than one – the interviewer also asked respondents to say which reason they thought to be the main one. Nearly half (46 per cent) gave 'checking eligibility' as the main purpose of the new claims interview and another 15 per cent said 'checking the claim form' (Figure 5.4). The latter response could have included a number of people who meant checking the form for completeness rather than eligibility but, even accounting for this and the seven per cent who said that they had no idea of the purpose of the new claims interview, it is clear that over half of claimants recognised that the interview was a necessary step in determining the outcome of their claim for benefit. However, the fact that nearly 40 per cent apparently did not do so may be a more important finding in the context of Jobseeker's Allowance.

Figure 5.4 Perceived purpose of the new claims interview

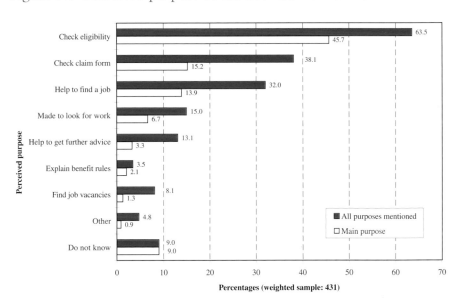

Around one respondent in seven believed that the principal purpose of their first interview with an Adviser was to find a means of getting back into work. Twice as many (14 per cent) emphasised the help that they might get from an Adviser as mentioned coercion (seven per cent). The advisory functions of the new claims interview tended to be noted as second order elements of the interview rather than as the main purpose. For example, in all, 13 per cent of people mentioned the interview as a gateway to other advice and four per cent mentioned advice on benefits, although the former was only singled out as the main reason by three per cent of respondents and the latter by none. Help with finding a job and being cajoled to get a job were also mentioned frequently as secondary reasons (but less often than advice); altogether 32 per cent mentioned help and fifteen per cent cajoling.

Respondents differed hardly, if at all, in their perception of the new claims interview according to their past experiences, although there was a hint that those with a history of casual work placed greater emphasis on the coercive functions of the interview; 18 per cent listed it as the main purpose of the interview compared with seven per cent of the sample as a whole. A similar proportion (17 per cent) of the small number of respondents with a history of self-employment also stressed being made to work but another third (35 per cent) emphasised help with finding a job compared with less than a seventh of all respondents (14 per cent).

The actual experience of the new claims interview, as recounted by respondents in response to a set of pre-coded questions selectively covering its content, was not greatly at odds with their perspective of its main purpose, although different in emphasis. Around two-thirds of respondents confirmed that they had been 'told about the rules on being available for work' and those 'on actively seeking work' (64 per cent and 67 per cent respectively; Figure 5.5). Since no-one thought to mention these as part of the role of the new claims interview it seems probable that, from the claimants' perspective, being 'told the rules' is construed as part of the process of checking eligibility; either that or respondents simply forgot that they had been told about the rules when thinking about the purpose of the interview.

With the exception of the Back to Work Plan, mentioned by 70 per cent of relevant respondents, no other component of the new claims interview was noted by more than a minority of the group (Figure 5.5). One in six people (17 per cent) remembered being told about in-work benefits (only 4 per cent mentioned this among the purposes of a new claims interview). Thirty-eight per cent recalled being told about 'how to look effectively for work', and nine per cent reported that they had been offered a job to apply for.

Figure 5.5 Content of new claims interview

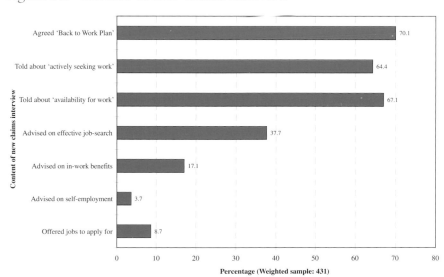

Percentage (Weighted sample: 431)

As one might expect, claimants' experience of a new claims interview and what they thought was its purpose were related to each other. Most strikingly, the small number of respondents who were given a job to apply for were much more likely to cite help with getting a job to be one of the purposes of the interview (38 per cent did so compared with only 12 per cent of other respondents). But people who remembered being told about effective job-search were also somewhat more likely than most to include help with getting a job among the objectives of the interview (18 per cent compared to ten per cent); equally, though, more of this group (11 per cent as against four per cent) noted the coercive aspects of being made to get a job which serves to emphasise the fine balance between these components of the job specification of New Claims Advisers. More generally, respondents who could report any of the content of their new claims interview were also more likely to have some comprehension as to its purpose.

If claimants' appreciation of the purpose of a new claims interview was influenced by their experience of having one, so the content of the interview affected their view as to its value. Respondents were asked whether the 'Adviser helped them to decide on the sorts of work to look for' and whether, at the end of the interview, they had a 'clear understanding' of what they 'were expected to do to find work'. Largely negative answers to the first question were offset by a largely confident, positive response to the second which, in turn, seems to have been associated with respondents' memories of the content of their new claims interview.

Almost one person in every four (23 per cent) felt that the Adviser had helped them decide on the sorts of work to look for. Most (53 per cent) of those who said that they had not been helped were unspecific about why this was so, but the largest group among those who did provide details (comprising 29 per cent of those giving a negative response) had already decided on the kind of work to look for. Ten per cent said that the reason why the interview had not aided them in their choice of work was that the Adviser had not discussed the matter, while a smaller number (seven per cent) said any discussion had simply not helped.

Respondents who were least specific about the reason why they had not found the new claims interview helpful were also more likely to say that most of the elements of advice and assistance had been missing from their interview. This may be true, though equally it could be a matter of recall; perhaps all the questions asked picked up an underlying negativity amongst this group of respondents. In contrast those who found the interview did help them also tended more often than other groups to remember particular components of the interview.

Whereas comparatively few respondents felt they knew better what kind of job to look for as a result of their new claims interview, 82 per cent were confident that they knew what was expected of them in respect to job-search. Moreover, this figure rose to 95 per cent for those who had been advised about how to look effectively for work and to 96 per cent for the 17 per cent who had received advice on in-work benefits.[3] Among those who had been told about the rules on availability and actively seeking work, 92 per cent also felt that they had a clear understanding of what they were to do to find work. On the other hand, around 40 per cent of respondents who could not recall this kind of input to their new claims interview were less confident that they knew what was expected of them.

A third (33 per cent) of respondents claimed to have taken any action as a direct result of their new claims interview. This was somewhat higher (37 per cent) for those leaving the interview with a clear understanding of what they were expected to do to find work. On the other hand, 35 per cent said that they took no action at all (and half of those with no clear understanding of what they were expected to do to find work) and 32 per cent that they only did what they would have done in any case. Those least likely to respond positively included people with a long history of unemployment, those without a previous job and the comparatively few respondents who have previously held a managerial position. The optimism in these findings is that people who could recall being given advice about how to look for work, or about in-work benefits or had been helped to decide what kind of work to look for were all disproportionately included among those who did take action as a result of the interview.[4] The range of topics that respondents remembered being covered by the interview also seemed to contribute to people taking positive action (Figure 5.6).

Under Jobseeker's Allowance the new claims interview becomes even more important. As of Summer 1995 when most respondents last applied for benefit, most claimants remembered the interview but felt that it had no effect on their behaviour. The seven elements of the interview portrayed in Figure 5.5 are ones that will be given greater priority under the Jobseeker's Allowance regime. But in Summer 1995 it was unusual for all elements to be covered in the new claims interview, or at least, made sufficiently salient. Most respondents remembered being told the conditions of receiving benefit but only a minority recalled the more pro-active elements relating to effective job-search or advice on in-work benefits. However, it was these elements which led respondents to change behaviour as a direct consequence.

---

3 Seventeen of the 18 respondents who had been advised to consider becoming self-employed also felt that they knew what was expected of them.

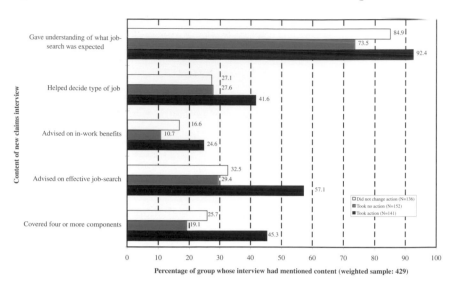

Figure 5.6 Content of new claims interview and subsequent action

Content of new claims interview

Gave understanding of what job-search was expected
84.9
73.5
92.4

Helped decide type of job
27.1
27.6
41.6

Advised on in-work benefits
16.6
10.7
24.6

Advised on effective job-search
32.5
29.4
57.1

Covered four or more components
25.7
19.1
45.3

☐ Did not change action (N=136)
■ Took no action (N=152)
■ Took action (N=141)

0 10 20 30 40 50 60 70 80 90 100

Percentage of group whose interview had mentioned content (weighted sample: 429)

5.1.3 Back to Work Plans   The aim in this section is briefly to consider how effective are arrangements governing the Back to Work Plan which is usually agreed during the new claims interview.

The first indication is that even among respondents who had first claimed within three months of interview, only 70 per cent of respondents could remember being asked to agree a Back to Work Plan, and 26 per cent said that they definitely had not done so. Clearly there is no means of determining whether this was the case, but the fact that approaching a third of respondents who had recently claimed benefit did not take the plan seriously enough to remember it imposes a limit on the effectiveness of the current system.

The official expectation is that almost everybody completes a Back to Work Plan, and the small number who began receiving benefit before the procedure was introduced should have done so subsequently. Therefore, respondents were asked about Back to Work Plans irrespective of when their current spell of unemployment began. Recent applicants and the more long-term unemployed did not differ in either the proportion who recalled, or who followed, their plan. The remainder of this section therefore refers to the full sample.

Respondents saying that they had not agreed a plan may include a mix of those who had not, and those who had forgotten. Generally, those not recalling a Back to Work Plan were no different to other respondents, with a few exceptions. First, the self-employed were marginally more likely to say that they had not agreed a plan: 26 per cent compared to 18 per cent for the

---

4   Least squares regression, not reported here, suggested that these three components of the new claims interview each had a significant and independent effect on the probability of respondents reporting taking action as a direct result of their interview, controlling for significant socio-demographic characteristics.

sample as a whole. The other exception was lone parents, 24 per cent who had not agreed a plan and 21 per cent, contrasting with the sample value of seven per cent, who didn't remember.

Fifty-seven per cent of respondents who recalled agreeing a Back to Work Plan had followed it unreservedly, and another 31 per cent either used it selectively or for part of the time. The high proportion who adhered to their plan might be expected: they would have been asked about their plan every time they signed on, at least in those offices with 'active signing' procedures. However, the fact that only 41 per cent of those who said that they had followed their plan also found it useful will be of interest in assessing the role of the Jobseeker's Agreement under Jobseeker's Allowance.

Perhaps not surprisingly, the only factors which seemed to discriminate between people who followed their plan and those who did not were former occupation and job history (Table 5.2). Respondents who had had a professional career constituted two per cent of the entire sample but 70 per cent of them claimed to follow their plan to the letter and another 25 per cent in part. At the other extreme, only 46 per cent of respondents who had not worked and 49 per cent of those never having a regular job followed their plan in detail. In each case 40 per cent adopted parts. Unskilled workers were also comparatively unlikely to follow a plan: 57 per cent did so, 34 per cent in part. These findings map neatly on to respondents' descriptions of their own careers (not shown in Table 5.2): those most likely to report sticking to the plan had never been unemployed before; or, else, mostly held steady jobs: those least disposed to follow the plan had spent time out sick or looking after the home or had work histories that were difficult to characterise. Similarly, only a half (51 per cent) of the self-employed abided by the detail of their plan and, of course, over a quarter did not sign up to it anyway.

Table 5.2 Responses to Back to Work Plan

Column percentages (weighted sample)

Reaction to Back to Work Plan	Socio-economic group									
	Professional	Managerial	Skilled non-manual	Skilled manual	Semi-skilled manual	Unskilled manual	Never worked	No regular job	Armed forces/other	Total
Followed it	61 (70)	45 (59)	45 (63)	41 (55)	42 (58)	36 (57)	33 (46)	38 (50)	[55] [(61)]	42 (57)
Part followed it	22 (25)	23 (30)	20 (28)	22 (30)	22 (30)	22 (34)	29 (40)	31 (40)	[22] [(23)]	23 (32)
Not followed at all	2 (3)	7 (9)	5 (7)	9 (13)	7 (10)	5 (7)	7 (10)	3 (4)	[8] [(10)]	7 (9)
Unable to follow	1 (1)	1 (1)	1 (2)	2 (3)	1 (2)	1 (2)	2 (3)	5 (6)	[4] [(8)]	2 (2)
Did not agree plan	11	19	21	17	20	19	18	12	[9]	18
Other	3	5	9	9	8	16	12	11	[3]	7
Count of people who agreed plan	(77)	(706)	(442)	(756)	(612)	(265)	(250)	(158)	(31)	(3,271)
Total count	89	925	626	1,019	677	413	354	180	34	4,486

Bracketed figures are percentages based on all respondents agreeing a Back to Work Plan

Figures for armed forces in square brackets, because they are based on a small number of respondents.

Almost half (45 per cent) of those who carefully followed their plan thought that it helped them. The self-employed who had used them had the least good things to say about them; 76 per cent did not think they helped, and nor did 65 per cent of the unskilled and 64 per cent of those who had been in and out of work. On the other hand, 53 per cent of workers older than 55 thought their plans to be of value, as did 51 per cent of people who had been on benefit for between two and four years.

A pattern therefore emerges. Back to Work Plans were less often followed by those with the most tenuous relationship to main stream employment, those with little work history, or who had spent periods outside the labour market. However, there was no clear relationship between following a plan and thinking it valuable; most respondents thought their plan did not help them find work.

Unfortunately, the reasons respondents gave for why their Back to Work Plan was of so little use were rather unspecific, despite extensive probing (Figure 5.7). Just under a third said that their plan amounted to no more than common sense; 17 per cent that they would have done the same things anyway; while 38 per cent said, simply, that it was of no practical value. Eight per cent thought that, given their particular circumstances, it was of little or no value, and five per cent took the more cynical view that a piece of paper was no substitute for going out to look for work.

Moreover, the reasons given for criticising Back to Work Plans did not seem to vary systematically. Thirteen per cent of respondents who had previously been in the professions suggested staff could do little to help, as did five per cent of the overall sample, a sentiment echoed by 12 per cent of people who had taken time out through sickness or home-making. Comparatively few respondents with a history of ill health (three per cent) complained that the plan merely contained things that they would have done anyway, as did the self-employed (three per cent) and, perhaps of substantive importance, those who had been unemployed for more than two years (seven per cent). But this was a cause of resentment among a significant minority of casual workers (20 per cent) and people who tended to be in and out of work (23 per cent).

Figure 5.7 Dissatisfaction with Back to Work Plans

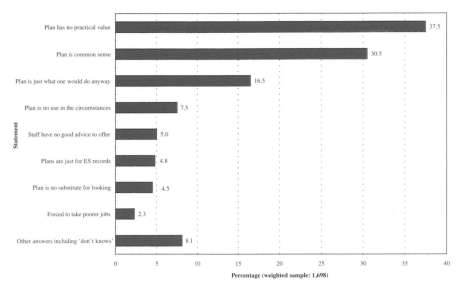

Nevertheless, there was also an intriguing pattern in the proportion of people who said that the Back to Work Plan was 'common sense'. This declined steadily with the length of a person's spell out of work, and the proportion saying that it was of 'no practical value', which changed in the opposite direction (Figure 5.8). The same phenomenon was reflected in respondents who had spent time out of the labour market looking after a home, among those who said that they had spent more time unemployed than working, and among those who could not easily categorise their work history. What these respondents may have been saying, well distanced as they were from the labour market, is that the guidelines did not take account of the impediments they see preventing them from finding work.

To summarise, most respondents could remember agreeing a Back to Work Plan, and the vast majority of those who did followed it at least in part. But in the main they did not do so because of any conviction that it would improve their chances of getting work. Most thought that the content of their plan amounted to no more than common sense. Those who thought otherwise, which included large numbers of people with little work experience, still frequently believed the plan was of no practical relevance. Respondents were generally abiding by the letter but not the spirit of the their Back to Work Plan since they had little faith that the plan was of any value.

Figure 5.8 Dissatisfaction with Back to Work Plans according to length of claim

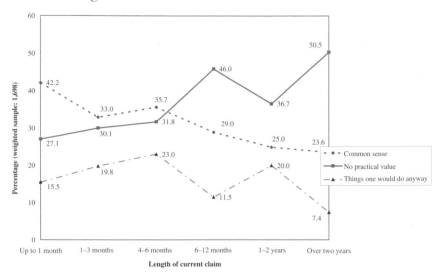

5.2 Signing on

While claimants have one new claims interview when they become unemployed, 94 per cent of them visit a Jobcentre each fortnight to sign on. The 'active signing' procedures increasingly used in Jobcentres are based on the premise that 'signing' presents an opportunity for staff to conduct a brief interview in order to check that claimants are looking for work effectively and to offer advice or exert pressure as appropriate. Judging by the survey, claimants are much more aware of the checking and policing possibilities of the signing on 'interview' than of scope for receiving assistance and advice.

In the discussion in Chapter 4 it was evident that, as clients of the Employment Service, respondents were not well informed about the rules and regulations applying to claiming benefit. When later in the research interview they were asked about the main reasons they were required to sign on, more felt able to respond positively to the question but, even so, no single response was offered by as many as half of the sample (Figure 5.9).[5] There was most agreement that the purpose of signing on was to check claimants were still available for work (46 per cent) and actively looking for it (34 per cent), and to enable benefit and National Insurance credits to be paid (32 per cent and 12 per cent respectively). Another 25 per cent saw it as an opportunity for the Employment Service to investigate whether they had been working while claiming. Only ten per cent mentioned being told about vacancies and seven per cent suggested that they might receive advice about applying for jobs. Moreover these perceptions were widely shared with little, if any, variation by the personal characteristics of claimants.

5.2.1 What happened at signing on

To provide a baseline for Jobseeker's Allowance, respondents were asked about what had happened when they last signed on. For those still on benefit, this would have taken place in the two weeks prior to interview in

---

5 Percentages in this section and in Figure 5.9 relate to all those people required to sign on in person.

Figure 5.9 Reasons for signing on

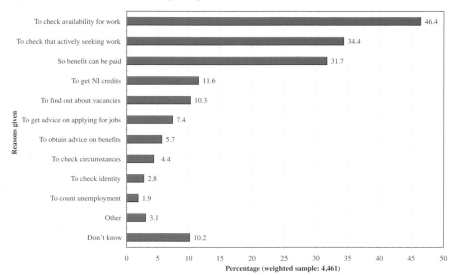

early Autumn 1995, although it would have been earlier for people who had already left benefit or who were not required to make a personal visit. Questions were asked about four elements of the signing on process which are part of the current active signing protocol but will be further emphasised with Jobseeker's Allowance (Figure 5.10). These covered enquiries made by Employment Service staff about job-search and the follow up of action suggested at previous interviews and also the provision of advice. In fact, fewer than half the respondents (42 per cent) remembered any of the topics covered, a fraction that fell to closer to a third among former professional people (32 per cent), skilled manual workers (34 per cent), people with a history of casual work (36 per cent) and couples living together without children (34 per cent), and to as low as a quarter (27 per cent) among the 100 claimants who were living with non-relatives.

Figure 5.10 Content of signing on

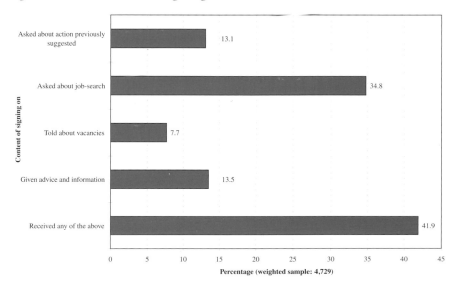

Thirty-five per cent said that they had been asked what they had been doing to look for a job, but only 13 per cent had been quizzed about their response to earlier suggestions. Thirteen per cent had been given advice or information and just seven per cent recalled being told about job vacancies. Certain types of claimant were more likely to have been asked, or to remember having been asked, about their job-search activities but the differences generally were small. The principal exception was between respondents who had worked in the professions, only 22 per cent of whom had been asked about looking for work and 11 per cent about follow-up action, and skilled and partly skilled manual workers, 39 per cent of whom were requested to say what they had done to find work and 15 per cent asked questions following up earlier agreements. This contrast is supported by a similar distinction relating to qualifications: 39 per cent of respondents without qualifications or with vocational ones were asked about job-search compared with 28 per cent of those with academic characteristics.

If it is assumed these differences reflect the content of respondents' last signing (rather than lapses in memory) then staff in Autumn 1995 may have been focusing their attention on moderately skilled manual workers, rather than the highly qualified. They may also have targeted people with a history of sickness and injury, 51 per cent of whom were asked about their job-search activities, and perhaps lone parents, since 41 per cent remembered questions about job-search (although the number of lone parents in the weighted sample is quite small (131)). On the other hand, despite the existence of a number of policy measures that become available as the length of a person's claim increases, there was no evidence that staff were adjusting their approach according to the duration of award. Possibly in response to labour market conditions, staff may have been giving less attention to the skilled non-manual who appeared to be marginally less likely to have been asked about jobseeking (27 per cent).

Finally, mention should be made of the marginal, though statistically significant differences between respondents who had managed to move off benefit and those who had not, which will be further investigated in later reports (Figure 5.11). Respondents who had moved off benefit were more likely to report pro-active intervention at their last signing on than those who had not. It is impossible, at this stage, to say whether this was a cause or whether, for example, a person's last signing is different from previous ones because of the more immediate prospect of them ceasing to claim. The fact that former claimants were, if anything, less likely to admit to taking action directly as a result of the discussion that they had had when last they signed on (36 per cent compared with 41 per cent), counsels against drawing straightforward conclusions.

Indeed, it is also important to note the potential importance of intervening variables such as local labour market conditions and the characteristics and management style of a respondent's Jobcentre. For example, respondents

Figure 5.11 Responses to signing on among current and former claimants

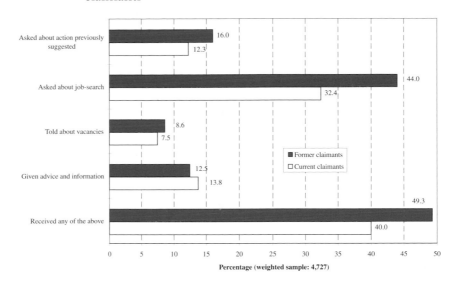

living in areas of high, and more specifically, moderately high, unemployment were less likely to report evidence of active signing. However, there were also differences between administrative regions. A higher proportion of pro-active interviews were reported in the East Midlands, the East, and the South-West (between 50 and 51 per cent) than in the North-East (35 per cent), Yorkshire and Humberside (36 per cent) the West Midlands (39 per cent) or London and the South-East (41 per cent). Within some regions, notably the North-West and the East Midlands, the link between the style of signing on interviews and local unemployment seemed to be maintained although the impact of individual offices became apparent at this scale of analysis. Indeed, the proportion of interviews in which at least one element of active signing was evident ranged from 17 per cent to 96 per cent (Figure 5.12).

Figure 5.12 Variation between Jobcentres in the content of signing on interviews

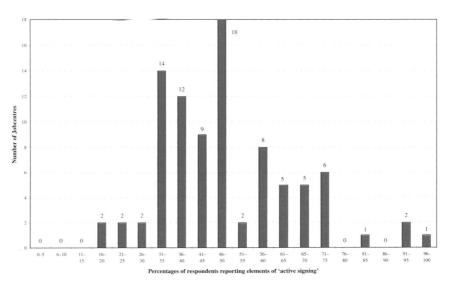

5.2.2 Responses to It is, of course, difficult to determine whether the content of the signing on
'active signing' interview affects claimants' job-search. Forty per cent of respondents who
could recall pro-active elements in their last signing on interview said that
the discussion affected their behaviour. Most dramatically 36 per cent of
those who took action applied for a job as a direct consequence of the
interview, 11 per cent for a training course and five per cent took a place on
Training for Work or Community Action (Figure 5.13). In addition, 17 per
cent looked at the vacancies displayed in the Jobcentre and 15 per cent
sought vacancies in the press, through agencies or by directly approaching
employers. Only two per cent reported taking more than one specific action
after signing on.

In a few cases the action taken following an intervention was related to the
nature of the intervention and the respondent's characteristics. Not
surprisingly people who had been told about job vacancies were more likely
than other groups to apply for a job[6] (41 per cent applied for a job directly
as a result of being told about vacancies). Similarly, people who took action
as the result of being asked about their job-search were over three times as
likely as others to look at displayed vacancies (20 per cent compared to six
per cent) or to look for work in other ways (19 per cent compared with
three per cent). Respondents given advice were more likely to apply for
training (19 per cent contrasted with four per cent) but less likely to look at
the posted vacancies (nine per cent rather than 24 per cent) or put in job
applications (27 per cent compared with 43 per cent).[7]

Figure 5.13 Action after signing on

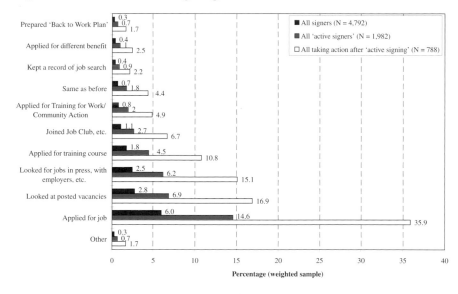

---

6   Sixty-seven per cent of those who took action as a result of being told about vacancies
    applied for a job compared with only 24 per cent of those who took action as a result of
    a pro-active signing on interview but who were not told of vacancies.

7   The series of questions following whether advice was given did not seem to produce any
    specific pattern of actions following the signing on interview.

Turning to respondents' employment record, twice as many former managers applied for unspecified training courses relative to other groups (22 per cent as opposed to ten per cent) whereas skilled non-manual respondents, just over half of them women, applied for Training for Work or Community Action (13 per cent compared with three per cent). Comparatively few (seven per cent) categorising themselves as having been in and out of work or more unemployed than employed seemed to go on training courses (measured against the sample standard of 13 per cent) although unskilled workers may have been more likely to go on Training for Work schemes (29 per cent compared with 14 per cent). Finally, those who applied for work following signing on included larger numbers of people who had never before been unemployed and people who had never worked; 56 per cent of the former group put in applications and 45 per cent of the latter, compared with 36 per cent overall.

To summarise, insofar as respondents gave signing on much thought, and most probably did not, it was about the Jobcentre checking up on their circumstances to see if they were still entitled to benefit. Very few saw signing on as a potential source of assistance or advice. These perceptions seemed consistent with people's actual experience of signing, when fewer than one in seven reported receiving guidance. On the other hand, a sizeable minority could remember features of the exchange at their last signing on, which might suggest that officers were using some 'active signing' techniques. Furthermore, the evidence points to some success in respondents' accounts of the actions they took as a result. (Whether they led directly or indirectly to people finding work is something that can only be explored when the second wave of data become available.) However, if we rely on the accounts of the survey respondents, it would seem that when most people signed on in Autumn 1995 the encounter with staff was perfunctory and involved little enquiry into what they were doing to find work, or advice and assistance to help them. That said, the evidence also points to considerable variation in the extent to which Jobcentres were implementing 'active signing'.

5.3 Client Adviser interviews and directives

Someone unemployed for six months is invited, under the Restart Scheme, to attend an interview with a Client Adviser at which a plan of activities is devised to help the person back to work. A shorter interview may take place after 13 weeks. While Advisers cannot insist that claimants take up offers of a job vacancy or training, an unreasonable refusal to do so could be taken as evidence they were not available for work and/or voluntarily unemployed. Under the more pro-active approach expected to be adopted under Jobseeker's Allowance, staff have greater enforcement powers and the link between compliance and benefit receipt will be emphasised. One might expect, therefore, a change in the role and effectiveness of the Client Adviser interview: this section is devoted to respondent's experience of them.

All respondents on benefit for more than three months were asked about the number of interviews that they had had with Client Advisers, and the outcome of the most recent.

5.3.1 Client Adviser interviews

Not surprisingly, the number of Client Adviser interviews that claimants had had increased with the duration of their award. Seventy-seven per cent of those on benefit for six to 12 months had had at least one, whereas a person in their third year on benefit would most likely have had four or more.[8] Interestingly, while it is generally assumed that virtually all unemployed people will be called for a Restart interview after six months on benefit, more than one in six (18 per cent) of those unemployed for over a year couldn't recall having an interview with a Client Adviser. There are, in the literature, anecdotal accounts of respondents seeking to avoid attending for interview and of claimants signing off benefit when one was due (Walker et al., 1994; White and Lakey, 1992). We have yet to investigate this but, of those who did attend, almost half (48 per cent) had found their last interview either 'very' or 'fairly helpful'; 22 per cent felt it had been 'not very helpful', and 26 per cent thought that it was 'not at all helpful'.

Figure 5.14   Frequency of interviews with Client advisers

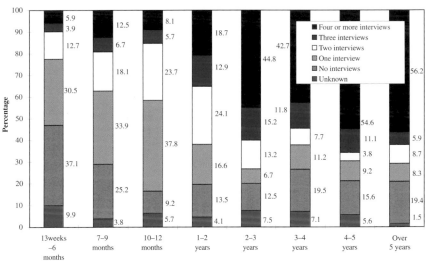

Older workers and, to a lesser extent, those with the least experience of employment and unemployment found the interview most helpful. Twenty-one per cent of people aged 55 or older considered that the interview had been very helpful (compared with a sample proportion of 14 per cent), as did 22 per cent of those who found their employment history difficult to categorise. The reaction of people who had not been unemployed before, or who had mostly held steady jobs, was more muted, but 51 per cent rated the

---

8   Forty-four per cent of people who had been unemployed for between three and four
    years had had four interviews or more, but 19 per cent claimed never to have had an
    interview with an employment adviser and eight per cent were unsure.

interview as being 'very' or 'fairly helpful' and only 21 per cent as 'not helpful'. The most critical were those who had been in and out of work, 54 per cent of whom thought it not very helpful or worse, and those who had had mostly casual jobs, 52 per cent of whom felt the same. The other fierce critics were former managers and, especially, the small number of people from the professions: 55 per cent and 80 per cent respectively found the interview either 'not helpful', or 'not very helpful'.

Accounts of the action taken as a result of the interview with a Client Adviser were mixed. Forty-two per cent claimed to have done nothing as a result of the interview while another 15 per cent said that they did exactly the same as they had been doing before. Nevertheless, the interview caused 43 per cent of respondents to change their behaviour. Other research has demonstrated that people who remain unemployed for long periods are different in a number of respects from those who return to work quickly (Payne and Payne, 1994; Shaw et al., 1996) which means that the clientele of these different kinds of interview will also vary.

Figure 5.15   Response to Client Adviser interviews

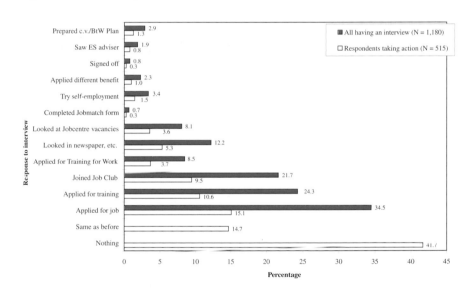

Of those who did take action after their interview with a Claimant Adviser, 35 per cent applied for a job, 24 per cent applied for training, 22 per cent joined a Job Club and 20 per cent looked for work in various ways. Only 13 per cent of people did more than one thing. These respondents were presented opportunities and responded positively to the intervention of the Client Adviser and, indeed, they were under some compulsion to do so. Training and Job Clubs are examples of activities which some unemployed may not be able to do by themselves without specialist assistance and therefore constitute positive, additional resources placed at their disposal. On the other hand, the more remedial function of the Client Adviser interview is illustrated by the fifth of interviewees who were motivated to do no more than they would normally be expected to do, namely, to look for vacancies in newspapers and on the vacancy boards or by approaching employers directly.

Respondents' reactions to an advisory interview did not seem to vary with the length of time they had been on benefit, and hence with the number of previous interviews. The proportion of people unaffected by the interview varied only between 50 per cent, for those who had been on benefit for three to four years, and 60 per cent for those on benefit about a year longer. However, comparatively few remain on benefit for this long so these estimates are not necessarily accurate. People who had spent less than six months on benefit had the highest probability of applying for a job directly as a result of an advisory interview (21 per cent), but generally there was no consistent pattern by the duration of a person's claim.

Indeed, it proved impossible to detect more than a handful of cases where the impact of an interview with a Claimant Adviser seemed to relate systematically to a person's characteristics. Receptiveness decreased slightly with age: 65 per cent of respondents aged 55 or over claimed to do nothing different as a result of the interview whereas only 53 per cent of under 25s admitted to this. A probable related difference is found between respondents who had previously spent time looking after a home, 63 per cent of whom either took no action after their interview or carried on as before, and those who had yet to have a career, of whom only 49 per cent behaved in this manner. Ex-managers were slightly less likely than other groups to apply for a job after seeing a Client Adviser (11 per cent compared with 17 per cent for the others), but they also tended to apply for training (15 per cent compared to nine per cent).

5.3.2 Training and directives

Acting as a gate-keeper, facilitating access to government training programmes, is a key Client Adviser function. Advisers can both advise claimants about particular training courses and direct them to attend. A third (33 per cent) of those who had been unemployed for more than 12 weeks had been advised to go on a government or TEC programme and in 44 per cent of these cases arrangements were made on the applicants' behalf. Not surprisingly the longer a person had been unemployed, the more likely they were to have been advised to go on a programme (Figure 5.16). Consequently the experience of respondents having an interview with a Client Adviser even though they had been on benefit for less than 12 weeks differs from other people. Only 16 per cent had been recommended to join a government programme: most are generally not available until claimants have been on benefit for six or more months.

This pattern was also influenced by the circumstances of the claimant. So, for example, 57 per cent of respondents who had a history of sickness had been advised to take up a programme, as had 50 per cent of lone parents. Differences by occupational skill level were not marked, but respondents with a history of manual work were marginally more likely to be recommended government programmes than were non-manual workers (35 per cent compared with 29 per cent), while the self-employed were the group least likely to be pointed in the direction of a scheme (23 per cent). Finally, it would appear that single people, including those living with relatives, were more likely to have a training programme suggested than, for example, couples without children (36 per cent compared with 26 per cent). This probably reflects personal characteristics more than living arrangements.

Client Advisers are not only in a position to recommend activities, they have it in their power to direct claimants to take training or do other things designed to get them back to work. How far clients of the Employment Service are able to distinguish advice from direction is a moot point. From the survey evidence it is impossible to know which is the more frequent. Questions were asked about four forms of direction (to courses, training programmes, programmes and residual category 'something else'). These suggested that more people had been recommended to go on a programme than had been directed to take up any single activity (Figure 5.16). Taken overall, however, 35 per cent of respondents believed that they had at some time been directed to do something which is the same order of magnitude as the number recommended for a government training scheme. Fifteen per cent of respondents had been directed to do more than one of the four activities listed and four per cent more than two. As with training programmes, the proportion of claimants directed to take specific forms of action increased with their time on benefit. Moreover, the 12 months threshold was very marked; whereas only 13 per cent of claimants who had been on benefit for between nine and 12 months had been directed to a training course and 15 per cent to a government programme, the corresponding proportions jumped to 32 per cent and 42 per cent for people who had been claiming for one to two years.

Figure 5.16 Advice and directives

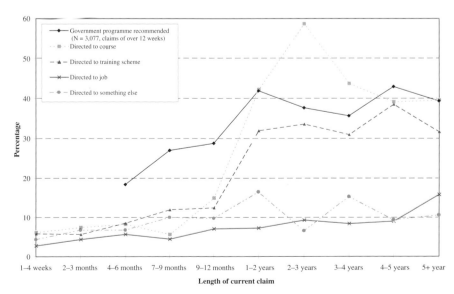

The precise instructions naturally varied from one person to another, but joining a Job Club was by far the most common strategy proposed: half of all those involved (Table 5.3). Seventy-seven per cent of those who said, possibly among other things, that they had been directed to attend a course were probably talking of a Job Club as were 56 per cent of those who mentioned a government programme. The next most frequently mentioned instructions were to apply for training or to go on a Training for Work or Community Action scheme; these were noted by 14 per cent and seven per cent of the respondents who had been told to take specific action.

Six per cent of all respondents reported that on some occasion they had been directed 'to apply for a certain job'. When asked to elaborate only 40 per cent reiterated that it had been a specific job that they had been told to chase up. Fifteen per cent said that they had been asked to expand the range of jobs that they applied for and 22 per cent said that they had been requested to join a Job Club. Twelve per cent were told to apply for training and perhaps seven per cent to look for jobs in some new way (although not all of these instructions were necessarily given on the same occasion). The most common action among those saying that they had been told to do 'something else' was also to go to a Job Club, followed by increasing the extent of their job-search and the range of jobs that they applied for.

Table 5.3 Instructions given to claimants

					Column percentages[9]
		Directed to:			All directives
	Training course	Government scheme	Job	Other activity	
Apply for job	–	1	38	13	10
Apply for wider range of jobs	*	1	15	16	7
Look in Jobcentre	*	2	3	9	3
Look in newspaper. etc.	1	1	5	15	5
Join Jobclub	77	56	22	35	50
Apply for training	9	20	12	10	14
Training for Work/ Community Action	4	16	3	4	8
Agree Back to Work Plan	5	4	*	3	3
Prepare curriculum vitae	*	2	2	*	1
Keep records	*	*	1	7	2
Base	409	570	303	361	1,643

* = less than 0.5 per cent, more than zero

– = true zero

Claimants who had been directed to do specific things were much as one might have expected on the basis of the outcome of interviews with Client

---

9 Columns do not add to 100 per cent because some respondents reported being told to do more than one thing.

Advisers (Figure 5.17). Seventy-two per cent of those who had been told to attend a course had been on benefit for more than a year and 40 per cent for more than two. Similarly, 68 per cent of those placed on a programme had been claiming for at least a year and 36 per cent for over two. On the other hand, the chances that people would be told to apply for particular jobs were somewhat less related to their length of time on benefit.

Comparatively large numbers of manual workers and people without qualifications were directed to training courses, as were a relatively large number of the small group of professional people included in the sample. On the other hand, former skilled non-manual workers (and hence women) were under-represented. Non-manual workers also disproportionately missed out on being sent on government and TEC programmes; these seemed to be more targeted towards people who had never worked and, to a lesser extent, towards manual workers. Respondents with a history of health problems, and lone parents, were also over-represented on training courses and government schemes (the latter to a lesser extent). Those with health problems were a (high) 25 per cent of the sample, whereas lone parents were just 1.5 per cent of the total sample; however without knowing more about these courses, it is difficult to understand why this should have been the case. Couples without children were less likely than most people to be sent on training courses, as were people aged under 25 (which may reflect a shared pattern of circumstances).

Respondents who were instructed to apply for particular jobs included relatively large numbers of people who had not previously worked, claimants without qualifications, and others who usually worked in semi-skilled or unskilled manual jobs. The same groups were also more likely to be told to do something else, such as looking for work in particular ways, or to expand the kind of job that they were seeking. So, too, were people who had a history of casual jobs.

To recap, Client Adviser interviews are a regular experience for most long-term unemployed claimants. The survey suggested that they were variously received by claimants, about half finding them to be of some help, while others, some with a history of casual work and others highly qualified, were highly critical. While the majority of respondents claimed that they did nothing special as a result of the interview, around one in six applied for specific jobs as a consequence, one in ten applied for training courses and an equal number took positive action to look for work. Likewise, 33 per cent of all claimants had been recommended to join a government scheme during their time on benefit, 41 per cent of those who had been out of work for over 12 months, while 62 per cent of all long-term recipients had been directed to take a course or undertake some other specific activity. What effect these activities had in enabling people to find work cannot be established until the second wave of the survey is analysed. Nor do we know, with any degree of certainty, that expanding the number of people who are

Figure 5.17a   Characteristics of people directed to attend a course

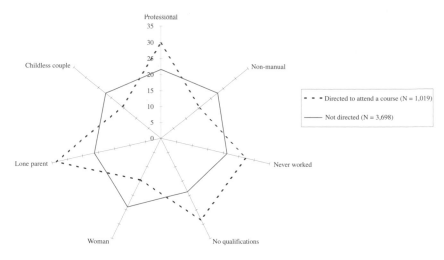

Figure 5.17b   People directed to go on a government programme

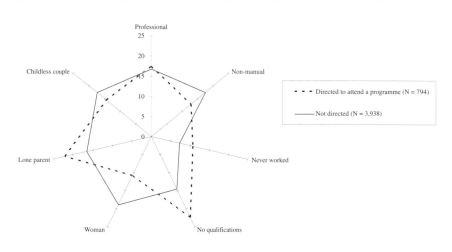

Figure 5.17c Respondents told to apply for a certain job

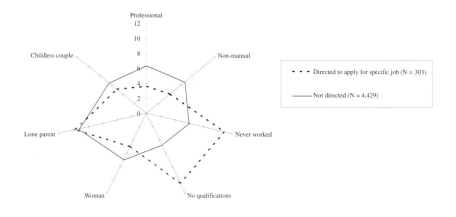

directed to take specific action by Client Advisers will necessarily mean that more people find work or, for other reasons, leave benefit. Nevertheless, it has been established that there is scope for expanding the role of Advisers, as is anticipated under Jobseeker's Allowance. Comparatively small numbers of people were encouraged into basic job-search activities while others were encouraged, or directed, on to training schemes and programmes that might prove valuable. It has also been shown that considerable numbers of respondents felt that they derived little benefit from their contact with Advisers and many took no different action following contact. Judging by results presented elsewhere in this volume (Chapter 6), most of these people will have been looking for work to the best of their ability, but some might well have valued more of the assistance that Client Advisers can offer.

5.4 Conclusion   This chapter has focused on the administration of unemployment-related benefits. It began with the initial application, considered the fortnightly process of signing on and the experience of 'active signing' before, finally, exploring the role of interviews with Client Advisers. The discussion described the situation as it was in Autumn 1995 and no account could be taken of subsequent developments.

The people most likely to benefit, in the first instance, from merging the administrative systems of the Benefits Agency and Employment Service are the small number of people who claimed both Income Support and Unemployment Benefit. Whereas most people needed to make only one or two office visits before receiving benefit, a disproportionate number of this group required three or more.

A significant minority of recent applicants did not recall the new claims interview though fewer among those with only recent experience of unemployment. Those remembering the interview emphasised the checking of their eligibility for benefit, noting the stress placed on being 'available for work' and the need 'actively' to seek it. Rarely were the seven components of the new claims interview, that were asked about, recalled by claimants. Moreover the more pro-active ones, which will be emphasised under the Jobseeker's Allowance, appeared to be the least recalled. However, it was these elements which seemed to relate most closely to respondents' perception of the value of the interview and to the likelihood of them taking action as a direct result of being interviewed.

The Back to Work Plan, completed at the new claims interview, is the forerunner of the Jobseeker's Agreement. However, very few respondents enthused about it. The large majority of recent claimants could recall agreeing a plan although over a quarter did not. Most people who remembered it, followed it to a degree but not with any confidence that it would do much good. Large numbers of people thought that their Back to Work Plan was no more than common sense and/or of no practical value.

Those who thought otherwise included disproportionate numbers of people with little prior experience of unemployment.

'Signing on', or 'signing', is a procedure that most of the unemployed repeat fortnightly. Because it is a routine it is possible that people think little of it, certainly the previous chapter suggested that they think little about it; this should alert the reader to possible errors in the recall of respondents. However, from what people could remember, signing on was primarily an opportunity for Employment Service staff to check up on claimants. In most offices, only a minority of respondents could remember any of the more 'active' elements being included the last time they signed on. Forty per cent of those who could said that it made a difference and over a third of these, 15 per cent of all who 'experienced' any active signing on and six per cent of all signers, applied for a job as a direct consequence of signing on.[10] It would appear, therefore, that there is considerable scope for further stimulating job applications by ensuring full implementation of the 'active signing' principles. Again, however, it has to be said that it has not yet been determined whether the additional applications resulted in more people being placed. On the other hand, the preliminary evidence presented above is encouraging.

Finally, there is the role of the Client Adviser and Restart interviews. Respondents were divided in their views as to their value. Some, more especially older workers but also those with little experience of employment or unemployment, found them to be helpful. Others, people moving in and out of work and from non-manual occupations, tended not to. Moreover the majority of respondents claimed that the interviews with Advisers brought about no change in their behaviour – no doubt, in some and perhaps in most cases,[11] because their behaviour was already exemplary. Nevertheless, despite these divergent views and negative perspectives it remains the case that over 40 per cent of respondents did say that they had done new things as a direct result of the interview. In a small minority of cases these things might be considered remedial, that is people started to undertake the basic tasks associated with looking for work. On rather more occasions it was doing something which could only have been done as a result of contact with the Adviser, enlisting for a training programme or, even, applying for a job suggested by the Adviser.

There are clearly practical and resource limitations on further expanding the role of Advisers. Even more pressing may be the need to learn more about the circumstances in which claimants do nothing by way of follow-up to an Adviser interview.

---

10 This is statistically equivalent to six per cent of people applying for a job each time they sign on.

11 See Chapter 6, Shaw et al., (1996) and Vincent et al., (1996).

6 LOOKING FOR WORK

Overview   One of the main aims of Jobseeker's Allowance is to improve claimants' job-search. Consequently, an important part of this evaluation is to record job-search activity prior to the introduction of the new system, and to measure how that system changes the type, frequency and success of job-search. Job-search activity is likely to change over time (Garman, Redmond and Lonsdale, 1992), irrespective of any intervention, so this aspect of the evaluation will need to make full use of the two-wave design. In this chapter, the emphasis is on establishing job-search activity baselines to which subsequent measures can be compared. Throughout the chapter, the weighted sample of all claimants is used.

The majority (93 per cent of 'current' signers) claimed to be looking for work at the time of interview, with a small number (two per cent) having secured work they had not yet taken up. In addition, most (89 per cent) of those who were no longer signing at the time of interview had been looking for work in the four weeks prior to knowing they would sign off.

This chapter aims to establish the motivation of claimants towards looking for work. It then describes the types and successes of their job-search activities. It also looks at the chances of moving off benefit, as viewed by claimants, and at the types of jobs they are looking for (or prepared to accept).

The structure of this chapter is therefore as follows:

- attachment to work (6.1)
- job-search activity (6.2)
- job-search intensity and effectiveness (6.3)
- flexibility and aspirations for work (6.4)
- prospects of obtaining work (6.5).

6.1 Attachment to work   The majority (93 per cent) of respondents who were signing on at the time of interview claimed that they were looking for work. This suggests that most claimants have a strong desire to work, but it is also worth looking at those who were not looking for work. To indicate respondents' attachment to work, they were asked the strength of their agreement or disagreement with the statement: *'If I had enough money to live comfortably for the rest of my life, I would still want to work.'* Almost 68 per cent of all respondents agreed, to a greater or lesser extent, with only 17 per cent disagreeing, suggesting that there is a reasonably strong attraction to work.

When analysed by respondents' current job-search status (i.e. looking for work, wanting work but not looking, and not looking for work), a statistically significant association was found: but the differences between groups were mostly small. For example, although 69 per cent of those looking for work agreed with the statement, so did 63 per cent of those who claimed that they did not wish to work.[1]

6.1.1 Respondents not wanting to work

Those who did not wish to work represented around two per cent of all those signing on at the time of interview. No statistically significant age or duration of claim differences were found between these respondents and those actively seeking work. The main reason, given by a quarter (24 per cent) of the 75 respondents who did not wish to work, was long-term illness. Around 13 per cent cited involvement in looking after the home. Eleven per cent did not wish to work because they were studying. Respondents were able to cite up to six reasons why they did not wish to work. These are shown in Figure 6.1.

Some reasons for not wanting to work might be considered more 'reasonable' than others. If these are genuine, respondents citing them are presumably prevented from working because of their circumstances. Nevertheless, the sample were all receiving unemployment-related benefits and, since they are unable to satisfy the required labour market conditions, their entitlement must be questioned. In the case of health problems, the degree of problem, and hence possible entitlement to other benefits, might be considered.

Figure 6.1 Reasons for not wanting to work[2]

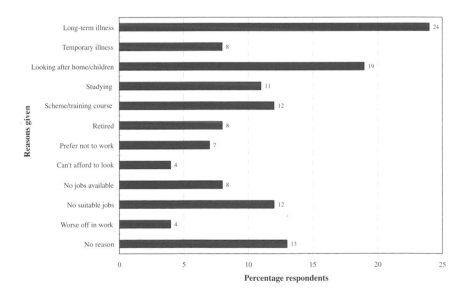

There are also a number of respondents apparently failing to meet the requirement to be actively seeking work without clear reasons. Only 17 claimants (fewer than one per cent of all signers) cited reasons such as 'prefer

---

1 Indeed, a strength of association measure (lambda) revealed little association.

2 The base for the percentages is the number of respondents rather than number of responses.

not to work' and 'no jobs available', but it should be noted that many of the 13 per cent of claimants who did not want to work but who offered no reason may also fall into these categories. In comparison with those looking for a job, claimants not seeking were more likely to be women and less likely to have qualifications. However, the small sample size prevents reliable comparisons being made.

6.1.2 Respondents wanting to work but not looking

Approximately three per cent of those signing on at the time of interview said that they would like to work, but were not looking. The main reasons cited were similar to those offered by those not wishing to work: temporary illness (23 per cent); on a government scheme or training course (18 per cent); and long-term illness (13 per cent). Again, respondents could give up to six reasons why they were not looking for work: in fact three-quarters gave just one reason and no-one gave more than four. These are shown in Figure 6.2, separately for men and women

Figure 6.2 Reasons for not looking for work[3]

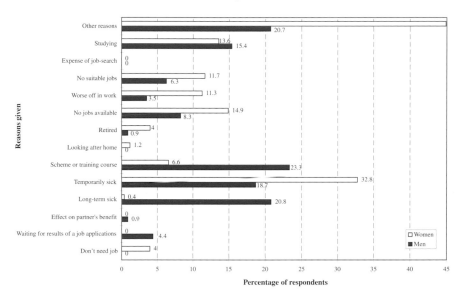

Note: the sample size for the chart is 96, of whom 26 were women.

A large number of respondents gave reasons that the questionnaire had not originally catered for. Almost half the women (45 per cent) gave 'other reasons', as did more than a fifth of the men. The most commonly cited options were those involved in other activities (studying or training) and those unable to work due to ill health:[4] men tending to state their health problems were long-term, and women short-term.. Others claimed not to be looking, despite wanting a paid job, because of a lack of jobs (nine per cent) or a lack of suitable jobs (seven per cent). A very small number (five per cent) felt that they would be worse off in work and some (one per cent)

---

3 The base for percentages is the number of respondents not responses.

4 This is a self-assessment of capacity to work rather than a recognised benefit status.

worried that their partner's benefit would be affected. Although these individuals appear to be breaching the 'actively seeking work' criterion, they represent a very small proportion of claimants. Whether similar numbers of such reasons for failing to seek work will be found in the second cohort remains to be seen.

Almost a third (32 per cent) of respondents who were signing on but not looking for a paid job at the time of interview had sought employment within the previous four weeks, suggesting that any inactivity may be a temporary state for some. Of more concern are the 19 per cent who claimed not to have looked for more than 12 months, over half of whom cited illness as their main reason for not looking for work.

6.2 Job-search activity

A principal aim of Jobseeker's Allowance is to ensure that claimants are actively involved in the search for work and to monitor that search. Consequently, this section focuses upon the actual process of looking for work. The vast majority of respondents (95 per cent) indicated that, to a greater or lesser extent, they considered it their responsibility to look for work. Three per cent did not express an opinion one way or the other and only two per cent felt that looking for work was not their responsibility.

6.2.1 Where are they looking for work?

With most claimants recognising their responsibility to search for work, what were they actually doing to obtain work? All respondents who had looked for work in the previous four weeks (or in the four weeks prior to signing off) were asked what they had been doing in the previous week (or the week prior to signing off) to find work. The proportions citing each method are shown in Figure 6.3.

Figure 6.3 Percentage of respondents using methods of searching for work

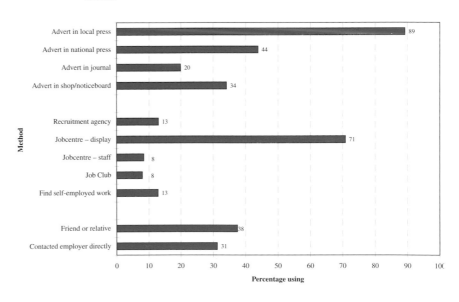

Base: those looking in previous four weeks, or the four weeks prior to leaving benefit.

The most common source of information was the local press (used by 89 per cent of respondents), confirming the findings of other research (e.g. Shaw et al., 1996). Display boards in the local Jobcentre (71 per cent) were also widely used. The national press was used by 44 per cent. Other local sources of information, such as shop windows and noticeboards, were used by around a third (34 per cent). Apart from Jobcentre display boards, which were typically visited twice in the previous week (median value), relatively few had attended a Job Club (eight per cent), or a private recruitment organisation (13 per cent), or obtained information from Jobcentre staff (eight per cent).

More appeared willing to take the initiative and adopt a more direct approach. Almost four in five (38 per cent) tried to find work via 'word of mouth' and 31 per cent made direct contact with an employer, either in person, in writing or by telephone. Those adopting this method typically made three such contacts, although some approached many more employers (60 being the highest reported). It will also be of particular interest to note how the intensity with which these search activities are carried out changes by duration of claim.

6.2.2 What factors limit their search for work? Although the desire to look for work may be strong, there can be factors which limit claimants' ability to search effectively. Just under 39 per cent felt that the costs involved in searching for work had limited their activity and an additional 14 per cent cited other reasons. Table 6.1 lists the percentage of respondents citing each limiting factor.

Table 6.1 Restrictions to job-search activity

Restriction	Number	Percentage
Financial limits		
Travel costs/fares	1,510	34
Postage/stationery costs	236	5
Clothing costs	68	2
Newspaper/magazine costs	142	3
Telephone costs	273	6
Other limits		
No telephone	40	1
No transport	283	6
No previous experience/qualifications/training	140	3
No suitable vacancies	215	5
Health problems/disability	191	4
Family restrictions	125	3
Criminal record	18	*
Location	118	3
Age	62	1
Wages too low	35	1
Base = 4,479		

* = less than 0.5 per cent

By far the most frequently cited limit was the cost of travelling to look for work, nominated by 34 per cent of those looking for work in the previous four weeks. Other financial limitations, such as the cost of postage and telephone calls, were suggested by relatively small numbers (five and six per cent respectively). Lack of transport was seen as a problem by six per cent. Factors which might have been expected to be more commonly cited, such as age (one per cent) or family restrictions (three per cent), were suggested by relatively few.

A number of people (four per cent) mentioned health problems and these were explored in some detail. When asked directly, 25 per cent of all respondents said they had a health problem or disability affecting the type of paid work they could do. This is a high figure, and compares with 15 per cent in the 1994 Employment Service Customer Satisfaction Survey (Nove with McKay, 1995). Of these, the majority (84 per cent) felt that the problem would persist for at least a year. The most common were found to be: problems with limbs, back or neck (11 per cent of all respondents); problems with the chest, breathing, asthma or bronchitis (six per cent); problems with the heart, blood pressure or circulation (two per cent); and difficulties seeing (two per cent) and hearing (two per cent).[5]

6.2.3 How well do respondents record their job-search activities?

Under Jobseeker's Allowance, claimants are expected to demonstrate they have carried out the steps in the Jobseeker's Agreement. This will involve keeping a record of their jobseeking activities to show they are 'actively seeking work'. Although similar rules previously applied, only 52 per cent of those looking for work kept details of their activities. On this evidence, almost half of claimants will be unable to satisfy this part of the contract and may run the risk of being unable to demonstrate their adherence to the Agreement.

6.2.4 What role can partners play?

When asked whether or not they felt they could offer assistance in their partners' search for work, 60 per cent of partners of main respondents felt that they could make contributions. Those partners with potentially more time on their hands, i.e. those in part-time work (68 per cent) or unemployed (83 per cent), were more likely to feel they could offer help.

Most help tended to be practical, such as looking for vacancies in newspapers (offered by 49 per cent of all partners), or at the Jobcentre (16 per cent), or asking others about vacancies they were aware of (15 per cent). A further 11 per cent said that they helped complete application forms or curricula vitarum. Fewer partners appeared to offer motivational forms of help, with just five per cent offering encouragement or maintaining morale and confidence. On the other hand, even smaller numbers (two per cent) resorted to more forceful tactics, such as applying pressure on their partner

---

5 It may be worth noting that the 1995 Disability Discrimination Act came into force on 2 December 1996.

to look for work. However, the use of an open-ended question might have interpreted as referring only to the practical side of helping.

6.3 Job-search intensity and effectiveness

The types of things claimants do to look for work were discussed in the previous section. This section considers the intensity of job-search and its effectiveness, as judged by positive outcomes such as interviews and job offers.

6.3.1 Strategies

Respondents were asked to indicate the extent to which they agreed (or disagreed) with a series of statements about applying for jobs. Table 6.2 summarises the responses. Around half (54 per cent) of the respondents felt that they would benefit from some help coping with job interviews, although a third (32 per cent) did not. However, the interview-to-offer ratios did not differ with responses to this question. In other words, those who feel that they need help with interviews are no less likely to achieve a job offer than those who do not.

The statement producing strongest agreement was the second: *'For me, it is better to work hard on a few applications than to do a lot of applications in a hurry'*. Three-quarters (75 per cent) of respondents who expressed an opinion agreed (either strongly or slightly). Only 12 per cent disagreed that quality was more important than quantity. Indeed, those who disagreed were found to have made significantly greater numbers of applications than those who did not disagree.

Table 6.2 Attitudes to applying for work

Statement					Row Percentages
	Agree strongly	Agree slightly	Neither agree nor disagree	Disagree slightly	Disagree strongly
'It would help if someone showed me how to cope better with job interviews'	24	28	16	18	15
'For me, it is better to work hard on a few applications than to do a lot of applications in a hurry'	43	32	13	8	4
'Getting a job is more down to luck than the effort you put in'	23	26	13	19	19
'Sometimes I get fed up and stop making applications for a while'	19	33	12	17	18

The feeling that luck plays a role in successfully returning to work was expressed by just under half (49 per cent) of those providing a response. Those more likely to cite luck as a factor were found to have been signing on for significantly longer than those who did not feel that luck played a part: the former had been signing on for 36 per cent longer.

Finally, as many as 53 per cent agreed that sometimes they stopped applying for jobs, having become disillusioned. In the following section, it will be noted that the intensity of submitting applications is unrelated to the duration of unemployment, but it would be interesting to gain an understanding of how individuals' attitudes change over a spell of unemployment. Data from the second wave of questioning will be able to address some of these issues.

6.3.2 How much time do respondents spend looking?

The amount of time claimants spend pursuing employment may indicate their dedication. The average amount of time involved in activities such as looking at job advertisements, writing applications, travel to interviews and visits to relevant agencies was six and a half hours per week (standard deviation 7.4). However over half (54 per cent) of the 4,208 claimants who provided a response spent four hours or less searching for work. Five per cent claimed to spend no time looking and three-quarters searched for fewer than eight hours. However, there were a small number who reported spending a considerable amount of time in pursuit of work. Around five per cent looked for 20 hours or more and one per cent for 33 hours or more. The maximum job-search time reported was 72 hours per week.

6.3.3 How many jobs have they applied for?

Another indicator of job-search intensity is the number of jobs applied for. Respondents who had looked for work in the previous four weeks were asked how many jobs they had applied for in that time. Figure 6.4 shows the proportion of respondents applying for different numbers of jobs, obtaining interviews and receiving job offers.

Figure 6.4 Job applications, interviews and offers in the last four weeks

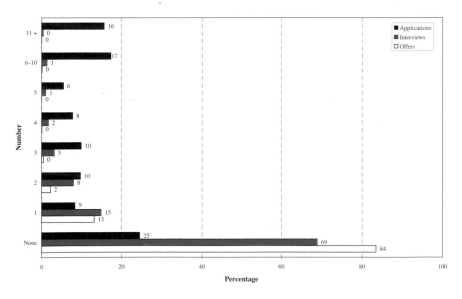

On average (as indicated by the median), claimants submitted three job applications in the four-week period. Nevertheless, this disguises the fact that a quarter (24 per cent) did not apply for any jobs during this time and five per cent made over 30 applications.

There was no evidence that the number of applications made varied with the duration of unemployment. This may be explained by those longer term claimants who respond to increasing frustration by applying for a wider range of jobs 'cancelling out' those who become more dispirited and reduce their application rate. Wave 2 will be informative.

6.3.4 How many interviews did they get? Over two-thirds of claimants (69 per cent) had no interviews during the four-week period considered. Fifteen per cent had a single interview and eight per cent obtained two interviews, leaving eight per cent having three or more interviews. As it has already been noted that many did not apply for any jobs, a more appropriate figure would be the interview 'success' rate of those who did apply. Of those who applied for at least one job, 40 per cent were successful in obtaining an interview but 88 per cent were unsuccessful in at least half of their applications. Five per cent of applicants managed to obtain an interview success rate of 100 per cent, of which a third (34 per cent) had applied for more than one job.

6.3.5 How many job offers did they get? More than one in three (36 per cent) of those who were interviewed during the period received at least one offer of employment. Job offers are, of course, less common than interviews. Most applicants (84 per cent) received no job offers at all. However, over half (52 per cent) of those who received at least one offer were in either full or part-time work at the time of interview. A small proportion (three per cent) had more than one job offer in the four-week period. Eighteen per cent were offered every job they applied for, although most (93 per cent) of these had just one interview.

6.3.6 Who has the best 'success' rate? Some people inevitably find it easier to return to paid employment than others. At this stage, some degree of success can be established by consideration of the ratio of job applications to interviews, and interviews to offers. Significant differences between interview success rates were found by duration of claim, social class and gender. Those obtaining the highest proportion of interviews per application were: those claiming for less than two weeks (18 per cent success rate on average); skilled non-manual workers (16 per cent); and women (17 per cent). Other factors, such as having qualifications, were not statistically significant.

For job offer success rates, statistically significant differences were obtained for duration of claim, qualifications, social class, and gender. The highest 'offer' success rates were obtained by: those claiming for less than two weeks (35 per cent) or between six and nine months (33 per cent); those with both vocational and academic qualifications (29 per cent); those in the managerial or technical professions (36 per cent) or those previously in the armed forces (32 per cent); and females (30 per cent).

These measures of job interview and job offer success rates are not presented as sophisticated measures. A more thorough analysis of success can be performed only once multivariate modelling techniques are applied, as will occur when the second wave of the data for the first cohort is incorporated.

The first part of this section will focus upon those defined as actively involved in job-search: that is, those who had looked within four weeks of the interview (if still signing on) and those who had looked in the four weeks prior to signing off.

6.4.1 Flexibility

Those looking for work were asked about the type of work they would be (or would have been) prepared to accept. Table 6.3 gives the number and percentage for each response.

More than three-quarters (78 per cent) wanted to work as an employee and just three per cent sought to be self-employed. Another 19 per cent said they were prepared to pursue both options.

Over two-thirds of respondents (68 per cent) who were looking for work in the four weeks prior to interview or had been looking for work in the four weeks prior to signing off wanted a full-time job. In addition, almost half (49 per cent of those looking for full-time work) of these said that they would accept part-time work if a full-time position could not be secured. Most of the rest (27 per cent of all) were looking for either full- or part-time work whilst just a small proportion (five per cent) sought part-time work only. These latter respondents contained a disproportionately high percentage of women (67 per cent), reflecting the evidence that part-time work is sought more by women than men (Garman, Redmond and Lonsdale, 1992). Part-time work was slightly more favoured by those whose claim had lasted between three and 12 months. There was no significant association between duration of claim and preference for working hours, although the second wave will enable a more thorough exploration of this type of question.

Almost three-quarters (71 per cent) said that they would be willing to accept a temporary position, whilst a further 13 per cent would consider this option. Forty per cent said they would accept any job, but there were variations by duration of claim (see Figure 6.5).

Although the proportion of those targeting a particular job did not change dramatically by duration of claim, the proportions of those prepared to accept any job or a range of jobs did. In particular, the difference between 'any job' and a 'range of jobs' beyond a claim-length of three years is much greater than for shorter durations. In fact, at the one- to two-year mark, more claimants are looking for a range of work than any job. However, as time progresses further, the emphasis shifts gradually to a point where, at five years and above, two and a half times as many claimants were seeking any job as sought a range of jobs. This suggests that those who have been claiming for three years and above show a marked tendency to broaden the range of acceptable jobs. This is presumably accompanied by an acceptance that they may have to take work they would not, in better circumstances, particularly want.

Table 6.3 Type of work acceptable[6]

Condition	Number accepting	Percentage accepting
Status		
Employee	3,470	78
Self-employed	116	3
Employee or self-employed	848	19
Can't say	6	*
Full-time	3,045	68
Part-time	200	5
Full- or part-time	1,226	27
Part-time if full-time not available		
Yes	1,506	49
Possibly	837	28
Short-term/temporary work		
Yes	3,150	71
Possibly	568	13
Specificity of job sought		
Particular type of job	1,262	29
Range of jobs	1,378	31
Any job	1,759	40
Can't say	25	1
Shift work		
Yes	3,309	74
Possibly	252	6
Night work		
Yes	2,772	62
Possibly	285	6
Weekend work		
Yes	3,320	74
Possibly	391	9
Work with variable hours		
Yes	3,731	84
Possibly	291	7
Work more than 40 hours per week	3,704	88
Living away from home		
Yes	1,724	39
Possibly	538	12
Move away from area		
Yes	1,578	35
Possibly	777	17

* = less than 0.5 per cent, more than zero

6   Valid percentages displayed, thus excluding missing responses.

Figure 6.5 Specificity of job sought by duration of claim[7]

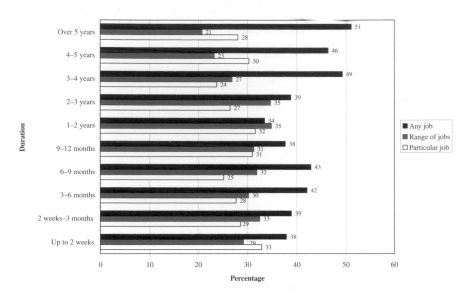

When it comes to the acceptability of different types of working conditions, most options elicited generally favourably responses. For example, 88 per cent were willing to work at least 40 hours per week and 84 per cent of respondents said they would accept work with differing number of hours each week (with a further seven per cent stating that they would consider this option). Similarly, both shift work and weekend work were acceptable to 74 per cent, with a further six and nine per cent respectively prepared to consider these types of work. A slightly less favourable reaction to night work was found, although 62 per cent were prepared to accept it with another six per cent willing to consider working nights.

Respondents were less prepared to live away from home or move to take up a job in another area. Only 39 per cent were willing to live away from home (a further 12 per cent would consider this option) and 35 per cent prepared to move away (a further 17 per cent would consider it).

Partners were generally less flexible in the range of work deemed acceptable for their partners. Whereas 84 per cent of respondents (including those who would prefer full-time, but would also accept part-time work) said they would be happy with part-time work, just 68 per cent of partners agreed. The same was also true of: temporary work (83 per cent of respondents; 69 per cent of partners); shift work (80 and 69 per cent); night work (68 and 54 per cent); weekend work (83 and 71 per cent); work with differing hours (89 and 83 per cent); work away from home (51 and 28 per cent); work requiring a move to another area (53 and 46 per cent). More disruptive types of work (e.g. working away from home and weekend work) seemed to be the ones with the largest discrepancy: partners seemed to be more concerned about this.

7 A respondent choosing the 'range of jobs' option is indicating a willingness to accept a variety of unspecified jobs.

Some aspects of job-search flexibility are related to such factors as duration of claim. In order to quantify this, an index of job-search flexibility was created, comprising responses to the ten items listed in Table 6.3. Each positive response was given one point, whilst a conditional response contributed half a point. Overall, the mean score was 5.9 (standard deviation 1.9), with an observed range between zero (indicating no flexibility at all) and nine (flexibility in nine of the ten items, or perhaps eight 'yes' answers plus two 'conditional' replies).

This scale summarises a great deal of information, but this simplification is both its strength and its weakness. It is likely to provide a more valid picture of flexibility than would fewer questions considered separately. However it tends to assume that all 'Yes' answers carry the same weight, which is unlikely to be true. For instance those saying they would take a job with shift work will include a range of levels of motivations: from those accustomed to such work, to those who would take it, but as close to a last resort. In addition, in this section, we don't consider how far those expressed views translate into actual job-search behaviour.

This scale may be used to evaluate some hypotheses regarding job-search activity. For example, it might be felt that longer term claimants may become more flexible in their requirements in order to secure paid employment. Figure 6.6 shows the mean flexibility score by duration of claim. In the main, the degree of flexibility demonstrated by claimants did not change much over time.

Figure 6.6 Job-search flexibility by duration of claim (maximum possible = 10; minimum = 0)

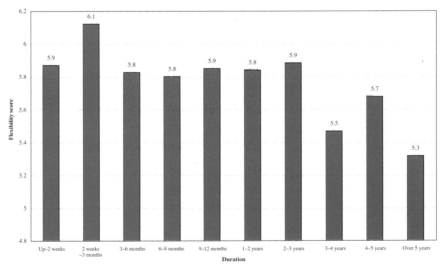

The peak between two weeks and three months may indicate the point when people realise they won't return to their preferred type of work immediately.[8] Perhaps the most significant aspect is the tendency for those who have claimed for over three years to be less flexible. Whilst this appears to contradict the finding that longer term claimants are more prepared to search for any job, the latter is a single measure whilst the scale is a composite of ten variables. Whilst longer term claimants were more willing to accept any job, they were significantly less likely to accept night work, weekend work and work involving differing hours.

However, it is worth saying that the scores varied a lot between individuals, particularly those unemployed for the longest times. This means that much of the difference shown in Figure 6.6 may result from chance. In fact whilst the difference is statistically significant, the difference itself is quite small. What we can say with certainty is that the longer term unemployed do not become more flexible in their aspirations.

However, it is equally possible that inflexibility leads to longer durations rather than being caused by it. The follow-up data will provide better evidence on this difference.

Job-search flexibility may also reflect local labour market conditions. It might be expected that claimants are more flexible in areas with higher unemployment rates. Figure 6.7 illustrates the mean index scores for groups defined by their unemployment rate.

The mean flexibility scores for those living in areas with all except the highest level of unemployment were not significantly different from one another, spanning a range of just 5.7 to 5.9. However, those living in areas with unemployment rates in excess of 9.9 per cent had a significantly higher flexibility score (6.2). It seems, therefore, that claimants living in areas with the highest unemployment rates had a tendency to respond to their local labour market conditions by reporting a more flexible approach to their search for employment.

6.4.2 Working hours   Respondents gave a wide range for figures for how many weekly hours they would be prepared to work. The minimum given was four hours; some were prepared to work as many as 120 hours. The mean was 46.5 hours (standard deviation 12.8 hours) and median 40 hours. Figure 6.8 shows the distribution of responses.

---

8 Claimants may restrict their job-search in the 'permitted period', up to 13 weeks according to background and qualifications.

Figure 6.7 Flexibility by unemployment rate

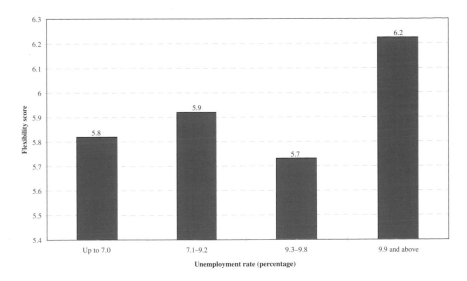

Only a small fraction (less than one per cent) would have preferred to work for a maximum that was less than 16 hours per week – the threshold for Income Support. The implication is that the vast majority are looking for sufficient hours to enable them to sign off. The most common maximum hours cited were in the range 36 to 40 hours, given by almost half (46 per cent). Significant numbers were prepared to work between 46 and 50 hours (14 per cent) and between 56 and 60 hours (13 per cent) and a few (four per cent) were willing to work for more than 70 hours per week.

Figure 6.8 Maximum number of hours per week prepared to work

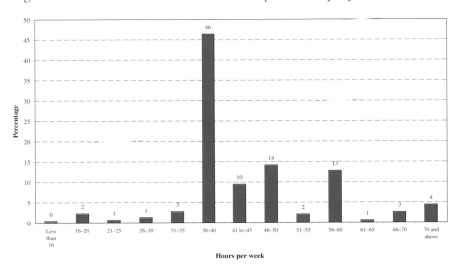

6.4.3 Expected and acceptable pay Respondents looking for work in the four weeks prior to interview or signing off were asked for their expected pay and, if this was unobtainable, their lowest acceptable pay. Figure 6.9 illustrates the distributions of both measures.

Figure 6.9 Expected and lowest acceptable weekly pay

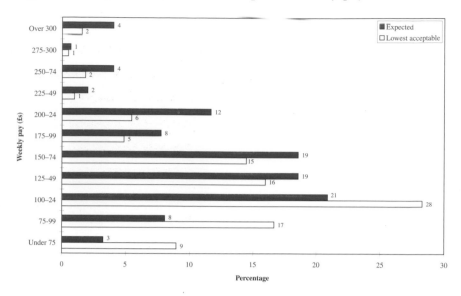

The mean **expected** pay for all respondents asked was £158 and the mean **lowest acceptable** pay £130. Given the small number of very high figures, the median values of £140 (expected) and £120 (lowest acceptable) are more meaningful and are comparable with, if slightly greater than, figures obtained in previous research (Shaw et al., 1995). The average expected pay is pitched at around £20 to £30 higher than the lowest acceptable pay. Indeed, although both expected and lowest acceptable pay peak at £100–24, the distribution for the latter falls away more rapidly than the former. A higher proportion of respondents' lowest acceptable wages are clustered at or around this point.

Expected pay levels and minimum acceptable pay levels can be expected to vary by social class. Wage expectations of different social class groupings are shown in Figure 6.10.

Professional people had the highest 'expected' pay and highest 'lowest acceptable' pay thresholds. Those who had never worked had the lowest expectations, closely followed by those described as partly skilled, skilled non-manual workers and those who have worked but not on a regular basis. The difference between expected and lowest acceptable wages was consistently in the order of £20 to £35. Those who had never had a regular job were prepared to accept a greater proportional reduction than any other group (£140 to £107 – a reduction of 24 per cent) whilst the least compromising were the professional people, who would accept a reduction of just 11 per cent on average.

Figure 6.10 Median expected and lowest acceptable weekly take-home pay by social class

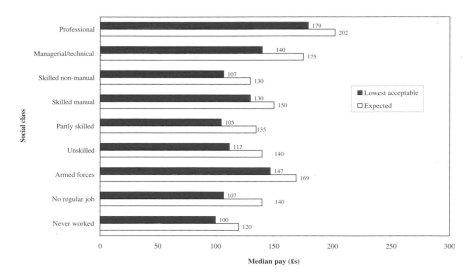

The idea of those wishing to return to work setting a 'reservation wage', in which claimants only search for work that pays at least as much as the threshold set, has been the subject of much debate. One argument for the concept suggests that the long-term unemployed set a reservation wage above that generally available in the labour market, and thus are unable to find satisfactory employment. The counter argument (Dawes, 1993) holds that this simply does not correspond with the behaviour of jobseekers. Analysis of the results of the second wave of interviewing will be better able to address these issues, but it was felt that a preliminary analysis of factors influencing proposed reservation wages was warranted.

It was hypothesised that the factors influencing reservation wages would be different for those with previous employment history and those who had never worked. Separate regression analyses were therefore performed for these groups, using a variety of socio-demographic indicators to predict the natural logarithm (due to the inherent 'skewness' of wage data) of the lowest acceptable wage given by respondents. With regard to those who had worked previously, the regression model produced was able to account for 24 per cent of the variance in the logarithm of reservation wages. Interestingly, the length of time that a person had been unemployed was not related to the level of the reservation wage, but several socio-demographic variables were. Those setting a higher reservation wage threshold tended to be: men; professional people or managers/technicians; older claimants; and those with both partners and children. Lower thresholds were set by those living with their parents or other relatives, who may be able to share in the resources of the other household members. These factors suggest two primary factors in the selection of a reservation wage: those governed by previous experience (e.g. those previously in more well-paid professions have a higher threshold); and those that are needs-driven (e.g. those with children choosing a higher criterion).

The regression model based upon those who had never worked also accounted for 24 per cent of the variance in the logarithm of reservation wages. Higher thresholds were associated with: men; older claimants; those with academic qualifications; and those living in areas of low unemployment. This model also found a lower threshold to be associated with those living with their parents or other relatives. The differences between the two models imply that those who have never previously worked are more sensitive to local factors, such as the unemployment rate, and to their qualifications. This suggests that the aspirations of those who have never worked may be set in relation to local labour market conditions in the absence of past earnings as a reference point. In their case, qualifications may serve a similar role to past employment in establishing a target threshold, and perhaps signalling their likely productivity to future employers. Detailed results from these two models form an Appendix to this chapter.

6.4.4 Concerns about signing off

Obtaining paid employment may signal an end to many concerns held by those without work. However, work can also bring with it new problems or exacerbate old problems, mostly concerned with money. When asked whether they anticipated any problems should they accept a job paying their lowest acceptable wage, 46 per cent of those who offered a response felt that they would have some worries and an additional six per cent thought they might have. Table 6.4 lists the problems cited by respondents.

Table 6.4 Concerns over signing off[9]

Problem	Number	Percentage
Losing housing benefit/help with mortgage	1,464	33
Not managing until first pay day	1,633	37
Not knowing how much money coming in each week	798	18
Having to pay back debts/loans/overdue bills	1,206	27
Having to pay for things get free on benefit	1,292	29
Amount of Council Tax have to pay	1,765	40
Having to wait for Family Credit	270	6
Having to wait for other benefits	197	5
Hassle of sorting out benefits	830	19
Wages being too low	1,826	41
Having to pay extra costs (travel, working clothes, etc.)	2,206	50
Having to sign on again after short time	1,634	37
Job being temporary	1,449	33
Job not being type of work wanted	1,291	29
Not being fit enough to do paid job	328	7
Someone else will be looking after children	111	3
Not knowing anyone to look after children	50	1
Costs of child-care	154	4
Base = 4,430		

9 The base for the percentages is the total number of respondents.

Two main themes emerge. The more common concerns respondents have about returning to work involve money. One-half (50 per cent) cited the extra costs involved in working, such as travelling to work or special clothing for work, as a source of concern. Many were also worried about their wages being too low (41 per cent), the amount of Council Tax they would have to pay (40 per cent) and about managing until the first pay day (37 per cent). Another main theme concerns the longevity of the work, as 33 per cent worried that the work would be temporary and 37 per cent were concerned that they might have to sign on again after a short time. These concerns were mirrored by the experiences of those who did leave benefit (see Section 8.2).

6.4.5 How quickly could people start work?

One of the measures of availability for work is how quickly people could start a job, if offered one immediately. Among the sample interviewed, 34 per cent said they could begin a job on the day they were offered, and a further 53 per cent said they could start the day after. Only small numbers gave other answers. Two per cent said it 'would depend', and one per cent that they were unable to start work if offered a job. There was a further nine per cent who said they could begin within 2 to 7 days of being offered a job, and only a very few answers (about 0.5 per cent) from those saying they would be able to start work, but would need eight or more days to do so.

A follow-up question tried to establish why respondents might take two or more days to begin a new job (three days if the interview took place on a Saturday), which amounted to 266 cases or around six per cent of the sample of unemployed claimants. No respondent gave more than three reasons, although they were permitted to provide up to five. The most common answers were:

• an expectation they would start work at the beginning of the week (i.e. on a Monday) (22 per cent)

• unspecified 'other plans or commitments' (19 per cent)

• needed time to obtain clothing or tools for work (13 per cent)

• needed time to arrange childcare (ten per cent)

• needed to go to Jobcentre first to sign off (nine per cent).

6.5 Prospects of obtaining work

Those signing on and who had looked for work in the previous four weeks (77 per cent of all respondents) were asked to estimate their chances of signing off in the next three months. Only eight per cent thought that their chances were 'very good', although a further 30 per cent thought them 'fairly good'. The remaining respondents (all bar the seven per cent who did not know) had a negative view of their job prospects, with 31 per cent believing their chances to be 'fairly bad' and 25 per cent 'very bad'.

Since unemployment varies across the country, we might expect location to influence perceived prospects of moving into work. Figure 6.11 shows the percentage of claimants signing on and who had looked for work in the four weeks prior to interview in each region who reported their prospects to be either 'very good' or 'fairly good'. Although each region had the same general pattern – with fewer than half the respondents believing their prospects to be 'good' – the effect is more pronounced in some. The South-West and North-East both contain a relatively low proportion of those rating their chances as 'good' and, consequently, a high proportion as 'bad'. Other regions, such as London/South-East and the East, have a much higher 'good to bad' ratio.

Figure 6.11 Prospects of returning to work by region

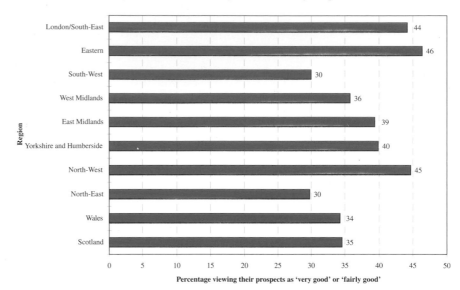

We may look more closely at the effect of local labour market conditions. It might be expected that those living in areas of low unemployment would rate their prospects more highly than those living in areas in which unemployment is more prevalent. However, as Figure 6.12 shows, claimants' assessments of their own return-to-work chances were not governed by the local level of unemployment. The ratings were similar for each of the three lower unemployment rate categories and the only slight difference occurred in areas of highest unemployment, where respondents were more pessimistic about their prospects.

Figure 6.12 Return-to-work prospects by local unemployment rate

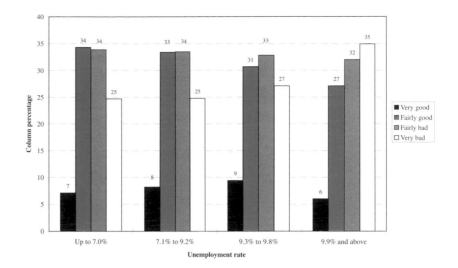

A series of analyses assessed how respondents' perceived chances of obtaining work compared with their perceptions of the *general* probability of finding work in their area. When asked to rate the chances of people in general returning to work in their region, just one per cent said they were 'very good', 17 per cent felt them to be 'fairly good', 46 per cent 'fairly bad' and 36 per cent thought the prospects 'very bad'. Fifty-one per cent rated their chances the same as those of people in general; a further 19 per cent responded in the same general direction but with different intensity (e.g. 'fairly good' instead of 'very good'). Around a quarter (25 per cent) rated their prospects more favourably than those of people in general; just five per cent rated themselves less favourably. It appears that most claimants see their opportunities for finding work to be at least equal to other claimants.

There was a statistically significant relationship between respondents' views of their own chances and responses to the statement: *'These days, finding some sort of paid work is not that difficult'*. Those who agreed that finding paid work is not that difficult also tended to have a more favourable view of their own chances of returning to work. Similarly, the relationship between the view of their own chances and the statement: *'These days, getting a job with decent pay is very difficult'* proved to be statistically significant. Those who held a more negative view of their return-to-work chances were more likely to agree that getting a job with decent pay is difficult.

The relationship between duration of claim and claimants who rated their chances more favourably (the 'optimists') and those less favourably (the 'pessimists') than the population is shown in Figure 6.13. In general, the longer the period of claiming, the lower the degree of optimism (although small peaks occur at two weeks to three months, one to two years and four to five years). The trend for those 'pessimistic' about their own chances is not quite so straightforward. The proportion of claimants with a pessimistic view of their return-to-work chances remains fairly constant: what trend there is suggests that a longer duration is accompanied by a slight increase in the prevalence of pessimism. It seems, therefore, that whilst duration has little impact upon pessimistic feelings of return-to-work chances, a longer duration is more associated with decreasing optimism. The overall trend makes intuitive sense. Those signing for longer periods may become less hopeful about their chances of returning to work.

Age, gender and social class were associated with confidence in finding work. Older claimants were less likely to have a relatively positive view of their chances, and over half of those aged 55 and over were pessimistic. Women had much more polarised attitudes than men. A higher proportion of women than men expressed positive and negative feelings about their return-to-work prospects. The social class categories that tended to view their prospects as worse than average were: managerial/technical; skilled non-manual; partly skilled and those with no regular job or who had never worked. On the other hand, more positive views were expressed by: professional people; managerial/technical (suggesting a degree of polarisation in these claimants); skilled non-manual workers; and those who had never worked (also a polarised group). These effects appear, in some part, to reflect genuine labour market phenomena. For example, the tendency for older claimants to feel that they will find it more difficult to return to work is likely to be based upon the evidence (see Shaw et al., 1996) that younger people hold a distinct advantage in the labour market.

Figure 6.13 Duration of claim by optimism/pessimism of own return-to-work chances

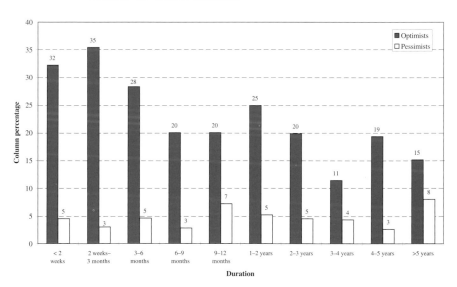

Partners were also asked to rate prospects of obtaining work locally. Over 85 per cent of partners broadly agreed with their (main respondent) partner, although there was a slight tendency for them to be less optimistic. Those rating their partner's chances worse than did the partner accounted for around nine per cent whilst the remaining six per cent were more optimistic.

6.6 Conclusions

The vast majority of current signers stated that they were looking for work at the time of interview. There was, however, a small fraction who seemed to have no good reason not to look and were clearly not actively seeking work. Others wanted to work but were not actively searching at the time of interview. Some claimed they were unable to due to ill health, though some had no clear reason.

The two main sources of job-search were adverts in local press and displays in Jobcentres. A number of factors restricting this activity were suggested, but by far the most common was the cost involved in looking for work. Partners felt that their main contribution to the job-search process was in the practical, day-to-day business of looking for vacancies. On average, claimants spent little time searching for work with over half devoting less than five hours per week. Almost a quarter were also found to have made no applications in the four weeks prior to interview. There was no clear relationship between the number of applications submitted and the duration of claim. The most successful at obtaining interviews were (independently) new claimants, skilled non-manual workers and women. New claimants and women also had the best job offer rates, along with those in the managerial or technical professions and those claiming for between six and nine months.

Respondents expressed certain views about the job-search process. Some wanted help with job interviews; many felt it best to concentrate on making a smaller number of quality applications. There was also a feeling that luck played a part in getting a job, and some reported becoming disillusioned and having stopped making applications, if only temporarily.

In general, claimants were prepared to accept a variety of types of work, although most preferred full-time work as an employee. Shift work, weekend work and work with variable hours were also acceptable to many. There was some evidence that those claiming for longer increased their acceptance of any job. Those living in areas of highest unemployment were the most flexible in their acceptability of working conditions.

More took a negative view of their prospects of an imminent return to work than took a more positive stance, and men appeared to have less polarised views than women. Older claimants were more negative about their prospects and differences were also apparent according to region of the country and local unemployment rates. When compared with the prospects of claimants in general, people tended to view their relative prospects less favourably the longer they had been claiming. Older claimants again viewed their relative prospects as poorer than did their younger counterparts. On the whole, partners agreed with the main respondents although there was a slight tendency for them to be more negative.

Few expressed a desire to work for fewer than 16 hours per week: the aim was therefore a job that would generally enable them to sign off. A range of salary expectations were noted, but professional people expected the most and had the highest 'lowest acceptable pay' threshold. Those who had never worked had the lowest expectations.

Appendix: Regression results for reservation wage

Regression results were discussed in Section 6.4.3. The table below presents a range of model and diagnostic statistics

Table 6A.1 Regression results for reservation wage

Variables	With previous work experience		Without previous work experience	
	Beta value	[t-statistic]	Beta value	[t-statistic]
Duration of claim (days)	-0.0125	0.86	-0.0084	0.15
Academic qualifications	-0.0643	4.01	0.1724	3.26
Vocational qualifications	-0.0073	0.51	-0.0712	1.42
Female	-0.2270	15.09	-0.1566	3.04
Local unemployment rate	0.0247	1.78	-0.1486	2.89
Professional	0.1223	8.24	n/a	n/a
Managerial/technical	0.1989	9.93	n/a	n/a
Skilled non-manual	0.0160	0.84	n/a	n/a
Skilled manual	0.0429	2.19	n/a	n/a
Semi-skilled manual	-0.0583	3.06	n/a	n/a
Age	0.1341	7.64	0.3173	5.54
Lives alone	0.0483	1.75	-0.0679	0.74
Has a partner	0.0053	0.23	-0.0691	1.12
Has partner and children	0.1516	5.29	0.0947	1.38
Lone parent	0.0117	0.70	-0.0401	0.85
Lives with parents/relatives (Constant term)	-0.1060	3.75	-0.2849	2.84
Number of observations	3,986		344	
Adjusted R-Squared	0.24		0.24	
F-statistic	81.23		10.97	

7 PARTICIPATION IN ACTIVITIES WHILST SIGNING ON

Overview · Claimants may, for a variety of reasons, wish to take part in a range of activities whilst signing on. Many will be keen to enhance work experience, perhaps to assist them signing off. Some are keen to obtain qualifications, perhaps hoping to increase their chances of a job. There are others who illegally use earnings from work to supplement their benefit. This chapter deals with all types of activities whilst claiming benefit, whether legitimate or not.

Following a brief discussion of what people do whilst signing on, this chapter deals with those engaged in paid employment (7.1), unpaid employment (7.2) and studying (7.3). Throughout the chapter, results are based on the entire (weighted) sample and thus represent a cross-section of claimants at the time of interview.

7.1 Paid work · When interviewed, 3,766 (80 per cent) respondents were still signing on. Most (91 per cent) described their main activity as 'unemployed and looking for work' and thus did not admit to doing any work or study. Just 132 (four per cent of those signing on) admitted to being in paid employment, all but two of whom were employed part-time. A further three per cent attended a government programme while less than one per cent were studying full-time.

In addition to those doing paid work at the time of interview, while signing on, a further 355 (nine per cent of those signing on at interview) claimed to have worked at some point during their current spell of signing. A number of those in work when interviewed (146 or 15 per cent of those in work at interview) had worked during their most recent spell of signing. Therefore, a total of 633 (13 per cent) respondents reported doing paid work whilst signing on.

Income Support claimants may work up to 16 hours per week without losing their entitlement:[1] the rules for Unemployment Benefit are more complex. However, some claimants may not fully appreciate the rules. When asked whether claimants were allowed to do paid work whilst claiming benefit, 68 per cent gave a positive response. Unsurprisingly, there was a substantial difference between those who had undertaken paid work whilst signing on, and those who had not. Just over 94 per cent of those who had done so knew that this combination was legal, compared with 64 per cent of those who had not – a statistically significant result. This suggests that

---

1 There are exceptions for child-minding, and those performing particular jobs such as coastguard, reserve army forces, and being a local authority councillor.

lack of awareness of the legitimacy of paid work whilst claiming benefit may prevent some from taking part-time work.

Six per cent appear to have worked and signed on, whilst under the impression that this was not allowable. These claimants will be considered in more detail shortly.

Figure 7.1 shows the weekly hours worked by the 132 who were in paid employment at the time of interview and still signing on. The numbers concerned are small so any conclusions are tentative.

Figure 7.1 Hours worked by those in paid work and signing on

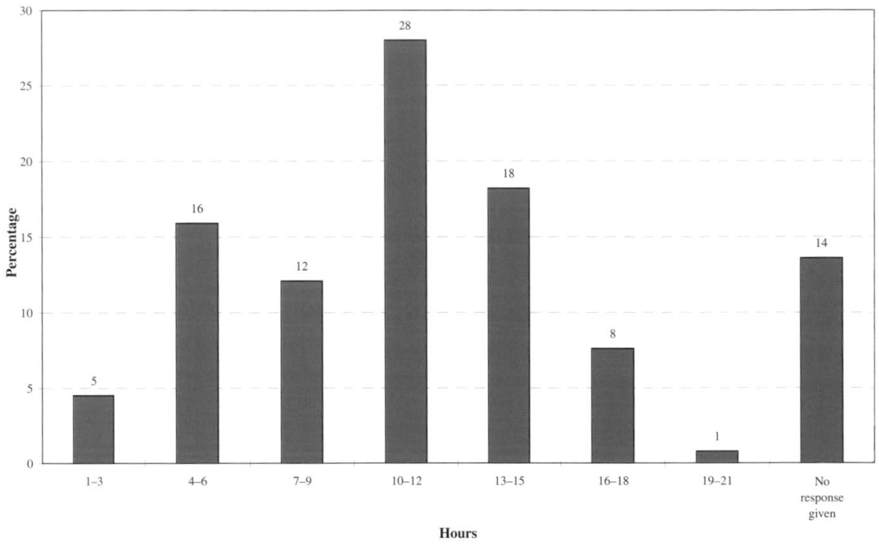

The largest number worked between ten and 12 hours per week (28 per cent) – the median being ten hours. Significant numbers also worked four to six hours (16 per cent) and 13 to 15 hours (18 per cent). The former group tended to work in areas often associated with low hours, such as child-care (31 per cent of those working between four and six hours per week), cleaners (14 per cent) and check-out operators (14 per cent). Claimants working the most common number of hours (ten to 12) tended to have similar occupations, such as the 19 per cent working as cleaners, but some of the other more common jobs were sales assistants (18 per cent) and taxi drivers (16 per cent).

Of particular interest are claimants who admitted to working more than 16 hours per week. Nine per cent of those working at the time of interview (12 respondents in the unweighted sample) worked more than 16 hours whilst claiming benefit. Mostly they were engaged in similar activities to those working fewer hours. All received at least one benefit (or National Insurance credits) suggesting that they are cases of benefit fraud or errors within the data. Cross-checks revealed patterns consistent with the former explanation being the more likely. Weekly take-home pay for those working more than 16 hours ranged from £10 to £80 (median £41) and all bar one were working as employees with no managerial or supervisory duties. That exception was a self-employed carpenter/joiner earning £80 per week and claiming both Income Support and Unemployment Benefit amounting to an extra £46 per week.

Fourteen per cent did not give the number of hours worked. This is a high level of non-response, but in such a contentious area a relatively high degree of non-response is expected. Some of these non-respondents may also have been working more hours than allowed under benefit regulations. Unfortunately, there are no direct means of validating this assertion as cross-checks with other variables (such as take-home pay and hourly rate of pay) also produced many missing responses. Assuming that all who did not state hours worked per week were actually working more than 16 hours, 23 per cent of those working and signing at the time of interview were employed for more than 16 hours per week. With this as a maximum, the true figure lies somewhere between nine and 23 per cent.

So who are those people who chose to work whilst signing on, and how do they differ from those who do not work? Table 7.1 shows the percentage of claimants in various groups who worked and signed on.

Women (17 per cent) were significantly more likely than men (12 per cent) to work whilst signing on. Although this may be a reflection of attitudinal differences, it is perhaps more likely that the work of those also signing on is by necessity part-time, and thus more likely to be either attractive to, or available for, female claimants.

Age differences were less pronounced. Similar proportions of claimants in each age group had undertaken some work in addition to signing on. Those aged between 45 and 54 years (16 per cent) were slightly more likely to do this than those younger or older (12 to 14 per cent) but these differences are small. More understandable are the differences due to duration of claim. The main difference is evident for those whose claim has been for three months or fewer (ten or 11 per cent) and those over this threshold (between 13 and 17 per cent). Part of the reason why those with claims of shorter durations are lower may be that these claimants are 'holding out' for a full-time position. When that does not emerge, some may be more likely to accept part-time work. There was no association between doing paid work whilst signing on and duration of claim.

Previous work experience made more difference. Those who had been mainly self-employed throughout their working life (21 per cent) and those who were mainly employed on a short-term basis (19 per cent) were more likely to work whilst signing than others (ten to 16 per cent). People in these categories are probably more able to pick up short-term work. At the other end of the scale, just ten per cent of those whose work history had been

Table 7.1 Personal characteristics of those who work, do unpaid work and study any time whilst signing on

			Cell percentages
Characteristic	Paid work	Unpaid work	Study
Gender			
Men	12	7	13
Women	17	12	16
Age			
Under 25 years	12	6	14
25–34 years	14	7	16
35–44 years	13	11	12
45–54 years	16	12	13
Over 55 years	13	11	5
Duration of claim			
Up to 2 weeks	10	8	12
2 weeks–3 months	11	9	12
3–6 months	15	9	11
6–9 months	15	6	13
9–12 months	14	7	17
1–2 years	14	9	18
2–3 years	16	10	16
3–4 years	17	8	12
4–5 years	15	11	8
Over 5 years	13	5	11
Work experience			
Mostly steady jobs	14	9	12
Mainly casual/short-term work	19	8	16
Lot of time sick/injured	11	10	10
Mostly self-employed	21	7	12
Never previously unemployed	13	11	14
Mostly unemployed	10	8	14
In and out of work several times	12	7	13
Much time looking after home/family	16	13	12
Social class			
Professional	14	13	28
Managerial/technical	17	14	17
Skilled non-manual	18	8	17
Skilled manual	15	7	10
Partly- skilled	13	6	11
Unskilled	8	4	10
Qualifications			
None	12	5	6
Vocational only	11	5	12
Academic only	14	10	15
Vocational and academic	16	12	20
All	13	9	14
Base = 4,732			

mainly characterised by unemployment worked whilst signing on. Presumably the same factors which prevented these people from obtaining regular, full-time positions (such as lack of qualifications, work experience) also counted against them when seeking temporary or part-time work.

The same reasoning may apply to the 'unskilled', a mere eight per cent of whom worked whilst signing on. This contrasts with the skilled non-manual, 18 per cent of whom obtained work whilst signing on. This too may be a reflection of the availability of the types of jobs (e.g. typists, computer operators, clerks, etc.) suitable for those signing on, i.e. typically short-term and with few hours.

Possessing qualifications also appeared to be associated with working whilst signing on. Those with both vocational and academic qualifications (16 per cent) and just academic qualifications (14 per cent) were slightly more likely to work and sign on than those with none (12 per cent) or with only vocational qualifications (ten per cent). Once again, this is probably a reflection of their relative abilities to obtain any work.

7.1.1 Does part-time work assist in the search for full-time employment

It is possible that part-time work enables people to maintain some contact with the labour market, and perhaps to assist in the return to full-time work. A clear majority (70 per cent) of those doing some part-time work believed it would help them get a full-time job. Just over one in five (22 per cent) thought it would not help. The views of those unemployed and not in any part-time work were quite positive, but not to the same extent. Almost two-thirds (65 per cent) thought that part-time employment might increase their prospects of a full-time job, whereas 30 per cent did not (plus a few 'don't knows').

7.2 Voluntary work

People take on voluntary activities for a variety of reasons. One of the principal reasons is that it provides another means of obtaining work experience whilst signing on. When asked to report any unpaid work undertaken on behalf of an organisation or other people, 395 (eight per cent) said they were doing some either at the time of interview or immediately prior to signing off. Almost three-quarters (73 per cent of those who had done some voluntary work) were current claimants, whilst the remaining 27 per cent were no longer signing on but had done voluntary work before signing off.

7.2.1 Number of hours per week engaged in voluntary work

The majority (87 per cent) of current claimants doing voluntary work gave their principal economic activity as unemployed and looking for work. A small proportion (six per cent) were also engaged in some paid employment whilst claiming and a quarter of these were working in excess of 16 hours per week when both activities were considered. Overall, those undertaking voluntary work spent an average of six hours per week (median value of all valid responses) on this activity. However, just under a fifth (18 per cent) did unpaid work for more than 16 hours per week. Whilst cases are treated individually, longer hours spent in voluntary activities could lead to questions being raised about claimants' availability for work. Figure 7.2 shows the number of hours spent on voluntary activities.

Most (77 per cent of whose who provided a response) who regularly did unpaid work spent between one and 12 hours per week in this activity. This reflects the nature of much regular voluntary work, such as fundraising or committee work (Gaskin and Davis Smith, 1995), which does not usually require much greater weekly input than this. On the other hand, some spent up to 50 hours engaged in voluntary activities and around two per cent worked voluntarily for at least 40 hours. In other words, there are a small number of claimants who are doing voluntary work on a seemingly full-time basis.

Figure 7.2 Hours per week in voluntary work

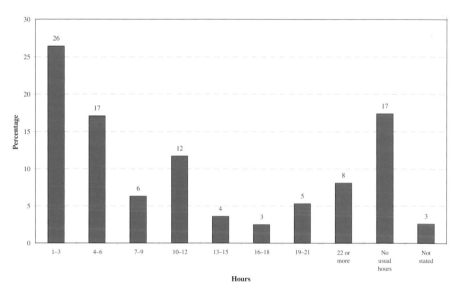

7.2.2 *Characteristics of those doing voluntary work whilst signing on*

It is worth exploring who were most likely to participate in voluntary activities (Table 7.1). Women were more likely than men to participate in voluntary work (12 and seven per cent of all claimants respectively). Professional people (13 per cent) and former managerial or technical workers (14 per cent) were also more likely to participate in voluntary work than those from other social class groups (mostly six or seven per cent). The duration of claiming did not affect participation in voluntary work. Perhaps the most notable links were with age and qualifications (see Figure 7.3).

Previous research (Shaw et al., 1996) has established a link between qualifications and taking part in voluntary work. In that study which was among a much wider group, those qualified to 'A' level or higher were much more likely to have done voluntary work than those less academically qualified. In both surveys, 17 per cent of those with 'A' levels or higher had done voluntary work, compared to seven per cent of those with lower grade GCSE (or equivalent) passes. Possession of academic qualifications (both with and without accompanying vocational qualifications) was associated with a proportion doing voluntary work. Five per cent of those with neither type of qualification, or vocational qualifications only, had done unpaid work – less than those with academic (ten per cent) or both types of qualification (12 per cent). It is possession of academic qualifications that makes the difference. Whether this is because those with a better academic record are more likely to view voluntary work favourably or whether their qualifications make these claimants more attractive to those recruiting volunteers is not known.

Figure 7.3 Participation in voluntary work by age and qualifications

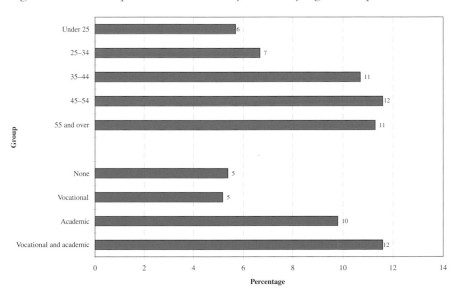

There is a clear relationship between age and participation in voluntary work. Those aged 45 and over (11 per cent) were about twice as likely to take unpaid work as those aged 25 and under (six per cent). This may be a reflection of a difference in attitude to doing voluntary work. A clue to this may be the relationship between age and perceptions of the use of voluntary activities as a means of obtaining full-time work (see Figure 7.4).

Among the whole sample, older respondents were less likely to view voluntary work as helping return to full-time work, and more likely to have no effect on their prospects. Whereas 45 per cent of those aged 25 and under felt that unpaid work could help their job prospects, this figure falls to 25 per cent for those aged 55 and over. Whilst more people in general feel that voluntary work has no effect on chances of getting full-time work, this increases with age. Forty-two per cent of under-25-year-olds felt this way in contrast with 61 per cent of over-55s.

This suggests people do voluntary work for two contrasting reasons. Younger people, whilst less likely to do it, are more likely to view it as ameans of obtaining full-time work. Fewer older people see it as helping

Figure 7.4 Voluntary work as a means of increasing chances of full-time work by age

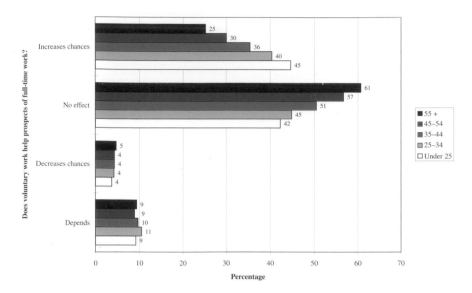

prospects, yet are more likely to participate: older people may therefore participate for the intrinsic value offered by the work.

7.2.3 Does participation in voluntary work assist in the search for full-time employment? In contrast to paid part-time work, fewer who expressed an opinion felt that voluntary work increased or might increase their chances of obtaining full-time work (38 per cent of all respondents). In fact, more (48 per cent) felt that it would have no effect upon their job prospects and just four per cent thought it might actually reduce their chance of a job. The remaining ten per cent felt that it depended on the situation. However, there is a statistically significant relationship between the perceived utility of voluntary work as a means of assisting job prospects and participation in this type of work. A much higher proportion of those who have done voluntary work think that it helps in the chances of obtaining full-time employment (54 per cent, compared to 36 per cent of those who have not). Fewer of the former group felt it had a detrimental effect (two and four per cent).

7.3 Studying Whilst claimants may study part-time whilst signing, only rarely can 'full-time students' qualify for benefit. Full-time and part-time are not defined in benefits legislation. If there is a doubt about whether a course is full-time or part-time, a decision is made by an Adjudication Officer who takes into account all the relevant circumstances, including any statement by the establishment which delivers the course.

Respondents were asked if they were doing 'any studying or education course' at the time of the interview, if still on benefit. Those not on benefit were asked about the situation just before they stopped signing on. Although fewer than one per cent gave their main economic activity as being in full-time education when interviewed, 637 (14 per cent of all respondents) were studying when interviewed, or had studied at the point just before signing off. Most of these (86 per cent) were current signers.

7.3.1 Number of hours per week engaged in education

The median length of time respondents spent attending a course of study (i.e. excluding personal study time) was nine hours a week, with a mean figure of 12 hours. Some (four per cent) studied for less than half an hour per week, 32 per cent for 16 hours or more, 19 per cent for 21 hours or more, and 12 per cent for 30 hours or more. The maximum was 60 hours per week. The distribution is shown in Figure 7.5.

Figure 7.5 Hours per week spent attending courses

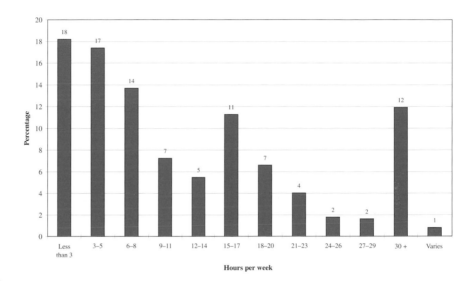

Few had long hours of study. However, peaks occur between 15 and 17 hours per week and 30 hours or more. Many of those attending a course for over 30 hours at the time of interview gave their main economic activity as a government scheme (44 per cent), the remainder being those unemployed and looking for work (50 per cent) and those in full-time education (five per cent).

7.3.2 Characteristics of those studying whilst signing on

Table 7.1 shows the characteristics of those who were studying whilst signing on. Mirroring the findings for part-time work and voluntary work, women (16 per cent of all respondents) were more likely to be studying whilst signing on than men (13 per cent). Study rates were found to peak among those aged 25 to 34 (16 per cent) and were lowest amongst those aged over 55 (five per cent), when any payback from training would be more likely to be shortlived. Previous work history was not associated with studying whilst signing on. However, there were some marked differences across social class. For example, 28 per cent of those classed as professional were studying whilst signing on, in contrast to ten per cent of the unskilled and skilled manual workers.

Perhaps the biggest contrast between those who were and were not studying whilst signing on was by existing qualifications. Just six per cent of those without qualifications were studying whilst signing on, yet 12 per cent of those with vocational qualifications, 15 per cent of those with academic qualifications, and 20 per cent of those with both, were studying whilst signing on. Unsurprisingly, those who were studying whilst signing on were more likely to be qualified. The question is whether possession of previous qualifications makes a claimant more likely to choose to study whilst signing. To answer this, just those studying at the time of interview were considered (i.e. excluding those studying just before the point they signed off). A significant relationship was still apparent. Six per cent of those with no qualifications were studying whilst signing on, in contrast with ten per cent of those with vocational qualifications, 14 per cent of those with academic qualifications and 17 per cent with both. Those having qualifications, particularly academic, were more likely to study whilst signing on.

Duration of claim was associated with studying whilst signing on. A higher proportion of respondents claiming for between nine months and three years were studying, than did those signing for more or less time. This coincides with the thresholds for some schemes which claimants must undertake after a certain period. These include the Restart Courses (introduced at 24 months) and Workwise (12 months for those aged 18 to 24).

7.3.3 Does studying assist in the search for full-time employment? Of those who responded, 56 per cent felt that studying whilst signing on increased chances of obtaining full-time paid work. Thirty-one per cent reported it to have no effect and 11 per cent felt that it depended upon circumstances. Just two per cent thought it had a detrimental effect. Responses to this question were significantly different for those who were and were not studying whilst signing on, as shown in Figure 7.6.

Figure 7.6 Studying and signing by perceived increase in chances of paid work

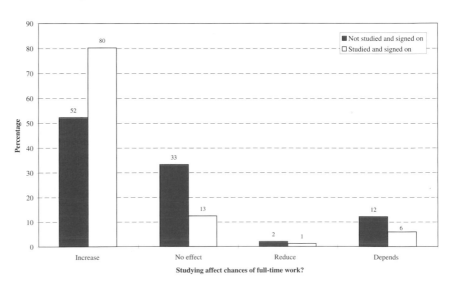

Eighty per cent of those who were studying and signing on thought that it would help to obtain a full-time job, compared with 52 per cent of those not studying. Far more of those not studying (33 per cent) thought it to have no effect than did those who were studying (13 per cent). Most of those who were studying whilst signing felt it would help them obtain full-time work. Some of those who did not study whilst signing on may choose not to because of the lack of any perceived utility, but many (i.e. the 52 per cent who think studying helps to obtain work) clearly had other reasons. Perhaps more likely in a number of these cases is the feeling that further training would be unnecessary: they may have been sufficiently qualified for their usual profession.

But does attendance on a course of study actually help claimants return to work? This question will be addressed by the next phase of the research. However, the first wave of data provides a simple measure. A number of respondents (20 per cent) had stopped signing on at the time of interview, having moved to another economic activity. It might be argued that if it can be shown that a higher-than-average proportion of those respondents who were in full-time work at the time of interview had studied just prior to signing off, then studying has an impact on successfully finding work. In fact, the opposite is true. Overall, 14 per cent of all respondents were studying whilst signing on, but this applied to just ten per cent of those who had moved into full-time employment. Of course there are many other factors, such as duration of claim, which will influence this type of comparison. Nevertheless no evidence has been provided to show that studying whilst signing assists the rate of returning to work.

7.4 Conclusion   This chapter has investigated various activities of those signing on as unemployed. Around one claimant in eight engaged in paid work or some course of study during their spell on benefit. One in 12 did voluntary work. In general terms, people who participated in these activities whilst simultaneously claiming benefit were more likely to view this as helping their job prospects. This was less true of voluntary work.

Most paid activities were for fewer than 16 hours per week, but some appeared to violate benefit regulations by working longer. Women were more likely than men to engage in paid work, and it was more common among former 'skilled non-manual' workers. Those with qualifications were more likely to work than those without.

Much voluntary work involved a commitment of few hours per week, although a small number worked as much as some in full-time employment. Possession of academic qualifications was linked to an increased likelihood of voluntary work participation and it was also found to be more popular with older claimants and women. Those who spent part of their claiming spell in study were likely to be more highly qualified. Women were more likely to study whilst signing on, as were professional people and those aged 25 to 34.

Overview
Jobseeker's Allowance will be judged a success, at least in part, to the extent that it creates a faster outflow from unemployment. This chapter looks at people moving off benefit. It looks both at moving off benefit in the short time between selection and interview, and at moves off benefit during the two years prior to the interview. It analyses which groups appear most likely to move off benefit before interview, and the destinations to which they move. The emphasis is on the most frequent routes off benefit, and particularly movements into paid employment.

The first section in this chapter (8.1) looks at moves off benefit between sampling and interview. Section 8.2 then considers problems encountered in moving off benefit, whilst Section 8.3 conducts some preliminary statistical analysis of lengths of spells on benefit. This section involves more sophisticated methods than are used elsewhere in the report, but which provide an insight into the types of analysis possible with a second wave of data. This chapter therefore looks ahead to future reports and analysis.

8.1 Moving off benefit prior to interview
Benefits for unemployed people insure against the risk of unemployment. In the Beveridge plan for a social security system it was assumed that the interruption to earning power caused by unemployment would generally be temporary, and, despite concerns about long-term unemployment, movements off benefit remain frequent. Almost 1,000 respondents (20 per cent of the weighted cross-section sample) had ceased signing on as unemployed after their most recent spell of signing and had moved into a range of different activities. This section looks at which groups were most likely to have left benefit, and at the sorts of destinations they went to.

Women were more likely than men to have moved off benefit between sampling and interview. More than one-quarter (28 per cent) of women had a spell doing something else after signing on as unemployed, compared to fewer than one man in five (18 per cent). This supports other evidence (e.g. in Chapter 2, comparing stock and flow characteristics) that men tend to stay on benefit for longer than women.

There was also a strong relationship between the age of respondents at the time of interview, and the proportion of each age group that had moved off benefit. More than a quarter (26 per cent) of those aged under 25 years had stopped signing on by the time of interview, compared to a fairly constant 19 per cent of those aged 25–54, and 13 per cent of those aged 55 or older.

As Figure 8.1 shows, women were more likely to have moved off benefit than men at all age groups. Men in the youngest age group had a greater propensity to have left benefit than older men. However age appeared to make less difference to the rate of outflow for women, excepting a much lower rate of leaving benefit for those aged 55 or older.

Figure 8.1 Moves off benefit before interview, by age and sex

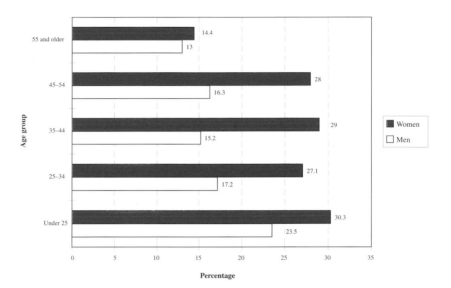

It is difficult to predict the effect of having children on the duration of benefit receipt among the unemployed. Households with children may have greater needs, encouraging job-search, yet households with children are more likely to have higher levels of benefit (chiefly through Income Support) which may mean that a higher wage is being sought, possibly prolonging unemployment. However, Family Credit is available to workers and should ensure that paid work (plus Family Credit) is more financially rewarding than Income Support. Moreover Housing Benefit and Council Tax Benefit supplement in-work income for those on modest earnings. In fact, the presence of children in the household did not appear to affect the rate of moving off benefit (prior to interview) for men. For women, there was a faster rate of movement off benefit where there were children aged over five years. However there was no difference in outflow between women without children, and those with at least one young (less than five years old) child.

Figure 8.2 Moves off benefit before interview and number of children.

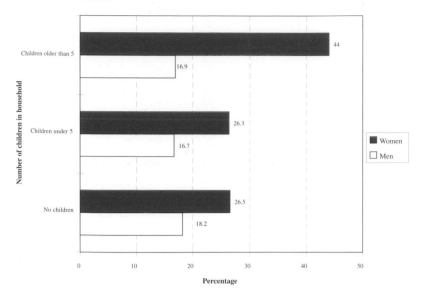

So far we have considered flows off benefit by characteristics of the person or household. In this section we consider the effect of previous labour market status. Interestingly, the occupational status of the person's last job prior to unemployment played no readily explicable role. Those whose last job was 'professional' were the most likely to have left benefit by the time of the interview (see Figure 8.3a), a result consistent for both men and women. However former 'managers', particularly men, were less likely to have left benefit prior to the interview. This element of white collar unemployment does appear a significant problem, as companies may have removed layers of middle and lower management in restructuring. By contrast, men and women formerly working in 'personal and protective services' were quite likely to have left benefit (often returning to those same occupations).

Figure 8.3b shows results by the industry of the last person's job. For men, those working in public administration, banking, other services and energy were the most likely to have moved off benefit. 'Outflow' was less common for men who worked in construction, manufacturing and transport. For women this pattern was evident, but less marked.

Figure 8.3a Moves off benefit and occupation in previous job

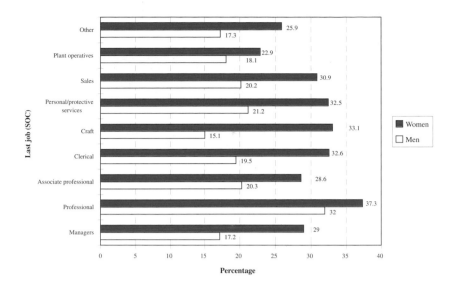

Figure 8.3b Moves off benefit and industry in previous job

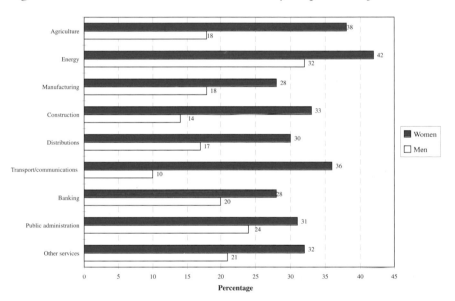

Part of the follow-up analysis will evaluate the impact of various Employment Service interventions. At this stage, any analysis must be rather cautious, since those moving into work may have different recollections from those currently signing-on. However a 'first look' may be instructive.

The initial conclusion seems to be that 'active signing' promotes moving off benefit, whilst the process of agreeing a Back to Work Plan did not. Those who received advice from an Employment Service office when signing on were more likely to have had a time off benefit (24 per cent compared to 18 per cent of those not given advice or information). However, only 19 per cent of those who recalled agreeing a Back to Work Plan had had some time off benefit, compared with 25 per cent of those who (said they) did not, but just 14 per cent of whose who couldn't remember. Clearly, the combined Wave 1/Wave 2 dataset will be more informative in this area.

8.1.1 Destinations

The previous section looked at the proportion of respondents leaving benefit before being interviewed. These departures could have been to any of a large range of economic status destinations, but the majority had moved into paid employment. A total of about half of those who had left benefit had moved into full-time work. A further 11 per cent had found part-time work of 16–29 hours a week, which is typically enough to disqualify them from further receipt of Income Support (there are exceptions). Moves into training accounted for a further 12 per cent of those who had stopped signing on, whilst moves into each one of the other possible destination states were quite rare. The full set of destinations for those leaving benefit between selection and interview are listed in Table 8.1, separately for men and women.

Men were more likely than women, among those moving off benefit, to move into full-time work, and more likely to start a training scheme. Women were much more likely to move into part-time work (27 per cent of women, compared to nine per cent of men).

Table 8.1 Destinations after signing on, by sex of respondent

Activity status	Men	Women	Column percentages Total
Full-time work	56	38	50
Part-time work (16–29 hours)	7	18	11
Part-time work (<16 hours)	2	9	4
Part-time education and part-time work	2	1	1
Full-time education	6	6	6
Government/TEC/LEC programme	14	8	12
Unemployed and looking for work[1]	4	6	5
Looking after home/family	2	5	3
Health problems	6	5	6
'Something else'	2	4	3
Weighted total (= 100%)	626	341	967

The same set of outcomes are analysed by age group in Figure 8.4. Younger respondents were the most likely to have moved into full-time work after signing off Unemployment Benefit/Income Support by the time of interview. Those older than 45 years quite often moved into part-time jobs. The option of moving into full-time education was most popular with the young, whilst those aged 55 or more had the greatest propensity to suffer from ill-health.

---

1 This is the respondent's own description of what they were doing after leaving benefit.

Figure 8.4 Destinations after unemployment benefit/income support
            by age group

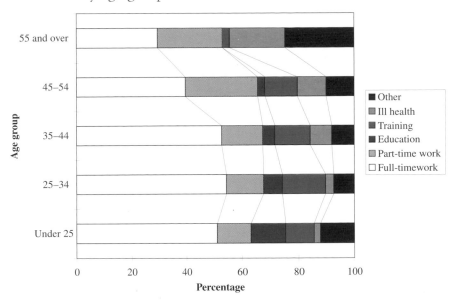

8.1.2 New jobs This section looks at moves into paid employment, which was the clear majority of those leaving benefit. Respondents were asked how they had heard of the job they moved into. The single most common source of information was friends or relatives, which accounted for 29 per cent of these new jobs. The next most common source of information was the local paper, used by 15 per cent of movers to find their first job after stopping their claim. A further 13 per cent cited the Jobcentre as the source of information, whilst 12 per cent had been successful after direct approaches to employers.

Respondents had moved into a wide range of different types of jobs that they found, but they were rarely high status. Only around one in six (17 per cent) moved into professional occupations. In fact more of those leaving benefit took clerical or secretarial posts alone, the largest category of these 'entry jobs'.

Further evidence of low status is shown by looking at job tenure. Almost one job in every three found by an unemployed person (32 per cent) was temporary, and a further one in six (16 per cent) was for a known fixed term. Fewer than half (44 per cent) of these jobs were in permanent positions. It is possible that temporary and fixed term posts go on to become quite long-term or even permanent. However employers may also terminate what are described as 'permanent' jobs. The follow-up data will indicate the duration of those jobs.

The remuneration offered in jobs may include certain benefits (or 'perks') as well as earnings, less than one-quarter (24 per cent) were receiving any of a range offered from a sizeable list of possibilities. A few received free meals (nine per cent). Most jobs were as employees (86 per cent). Just over one in ten (11 per cent) became self-employed, with a residual three per cent unsure of their employment status.

Respondents had moved into jobs with a quite considerable range of working hours. One job was for as few as two hours a week. One-quarter of respondents were working up to 30 hours a week. At the top end of working weeks, one-quarter were working for 40 hours, or longer.

A number of means-tested benefits are available to workers. Those working 16 or more hours a week can claim Family Credit, if they have children and their level of income and savings is sufficiently low. A new benefit, Earnings Top-Up, is being piloted for workers without children. Housing Benefit and Council Tax Benefit depend on financial situation and outgoings, without a test of working hours or a requirement that children are present. Only quite small numbers reported receiving any of these benefits. Just five per cent reported receiving Council Tax Benefit or Family Credit (eight per cent of respondents with children) and just six per cent Housing Benefit.

8.1.3 Other destinations *a) Training programmes and full-time education*
As mentioned above, only a small number of cases left benefit for training courses (N = 113 cases, weighted). In three-quarters of cases this was for Training for Work schemes. Of the remaining 25 per cent of cases, nine per cent were uncertain which course they had moved on to, and seven per cent went on to Community Action. The number moving into full-time education was also small, and the range of destinations quite diverse. The majority were pursuing vocational courses, although a notable 19 per cent were going on to study for a degree, perhaps reflecting when the sample was selected.

b) Other activities
The discussion above has looked at people leaving benefit to take up work, or move into education and training courses. A total of 155 cases gave other reasons why they stopped signing. Of these 46 (30 per cent) moved on to sickness related benefits. Seven per cent went abroad or took a holiday (presumably sufficiently long, or frequent, to cease benefit entitlement).

8.2 Problems leaving benefit Some previous research (McLaughlin, Millar and Cooke, 1989) has suggested that various problems complicate the transition from benefit into work. Some of these findings echo a government interpretation that:

> 'Research has shown that unemployed families are particularly concerned about how to get over the first weeks after out of work benefits stop but before first wages start.'
> (Alistair Burt in DSS Press Release 96/064, 2 April 1996)

Reforms from April 1996 include a four-week 'run-on' of entitlement to Housing Benefit and Council Tax Benefit, for job starters unemployed for six months or longer.

Respondents were asked, if they had moved off benefit, which of a list of 17 potential problems they had encountered. In exactly one-half of cases, none of these potential hurdles had been troublesome. For the remainder, the delay in receiving wages proved most significant (see Figure 8.5): this is one concern that the Back to Work Bonus is intended to tackle. Paying the rent, and additional travelling expenses, were the most common specific problems encountered. However problems meeting general living expenses were the second most frequent source of problems.

Figure 8.5 Problems encountered when moving off benefit

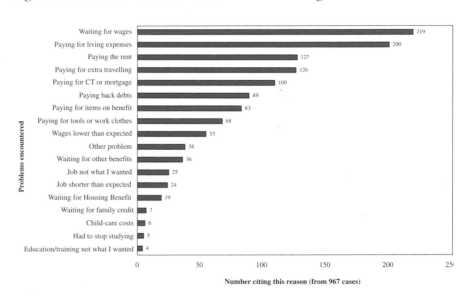

Some problems may be more serious than others, but there are few ways of detecting this given the data available. However we may still look at the number of problems mentioned. The overall average was 1.3 problems. Men were more likely to report problems than women, and reported more – an average of 1.4 compared to 1.1 for women. Fewer problems were mentioned by those at either end of the age range, than by those aged 25–54 years. Whilst these figures make interesting reading they don't address the question of whether people are dissuaded from taking jobs by the 'fear' or perception that they will face problems, which may be more significant. Section 6.4.4 has examined potential concerns.

8.2.1 Better off unemployed? Concern is sometimes expressed that people are better off 'on the dole' than in work. This is sometimes known as the 'unemployment trap', and exists if wages are likely to be lower than the money received on benefit. Alternatively, wages may exceed benefit income, but either the increase is rather modest, or the financial costs of working (such as travel costs) wipe out much of the financial gain.

If such a 'trap' does exist, it could lead people either to decline job offers, or indeed to become dispirited from job-search in the first place. However much of the evidence in this area is contested (Atkinson and Micklewright 1991). The motivation to take work may not be purely financial, for example. And benefit income may be reduced if job offers are declined or job-search is restricted. Therefore the 'unemployment trap' may be part of an overly simplistic view of the labour market.

In the main survey, those who had left unemployment were asked: *'Overall, are you now better off or worse off in money terms than you were when you were signing on?'.* This was designed to measure the 'net' situation, although the questions would not identify reasons other than leaving benefit for the change in money circumstances. Nor does it tell us about anxiety about leaving benefit. However, the majority, as shown in Table 8.2, were much or a little better off. But nearly one in five claimed to be worse off.

Table 8.2 Whether better or worse off in work

Better/worse off	Men	Women	Column percentages Total
Much better off	38	33	36
A little better off	24	21	23
About the same	15	16	16
A little worse off	8	11	9
A lot worse off	10	13	11
Can't say	3	3	3
Circumstances changed in other ways	*	*	*
Missing data	3	2	3
Weighted total (= 100%)	626	341	967

Base: those no longer signing

Men tended to give more positive answers than women. Two-thirds of men (66 per cent) said they were better off now they were not signing on, compared to 54 per cent of women. To some extent these differences must reflect the different destinations people had after leaving benefit and the different wage levels that different jobs commanded. More than eight in ten (81 per cent) of those leaving benefit for a full-time job said they were now better off: indeed 57 per cent described themselves as 'much' better off. Fewer than one in ten (nine per cent) claimed to be worse off in a full-time job than when signing on.

Satisfaction with living standards having stopped signing was closely linked to family status. Those without children were most likely to say they were better off than when signing (61 per cent of this group). This may be contrasted with fewer than half (48 per cent) of respondents with at least one child aged five or less. But those with older children (none aged under five) were much more likely to feel better off not signing on — 58 per cent thought this.

Table 8.3 Satisfaction with moving off benefit by claim duration

		Column percentages	
	Duration of claim		
	Less than two weeks	At least two weeks, less than six months	At least six months, less than one year	At least one year
Better off	71	65	39	42
About the same	10	15	9	27
Worse off	12	16	43	21
Other categories	7	4	9	10
Total (= 100%)	90	617	131	128

Base: those stopped signing on

Those on benefit for six months or longer were the least likely to feel better off when they stopped receiving benefit. Only 42 per cent of those unemployed for more than a year felt better off having left benefit. And more than one in five felt worse off (21 per cent). Table 8.3 provides a summary of replies. Those unemployed for between six months and a year recorded the worst changes after leaving benefit: those worse off outnumbered those who said they were better off.

8.3 A preliminary statistical analysis of 'spells' of signing on

As part of the interview, respondents were taken through a Work and Benefit History Sheet covering employment status, and whether signing on (or not), for the period between October 1993 and the time of the interview. It is important to appreciate the relationship between this data, and the method used to draw the sample. Figure 8.6 is a graphical representation that applies to the stock sample. The horizontal lines are drawn to represent spells on benefit, with spells off benefit being the gaps between those lines, for a few hypothetical cases. Individual A will not have been included in the sample, because he was not on benefit at the time of selection. However individual B would have been included. Notice that A and B started on benefit at the same time, but A had a shorter duration of unemployment.

Some of the stock sample may have left benefit between selection and interview: case D illustrates this. Other possibilities are those on benefit throughout the 'observation period' (C), if not earlier, and those with repeated spells of unemployment (E).

In some cases, unemployment will continue after the interview date (B, C, E). These are 'incomplete spells', whose final durations are unknown. By contrast A and D have 'completed spells' with known length.

Figure 8.6 Selection of the stock sample

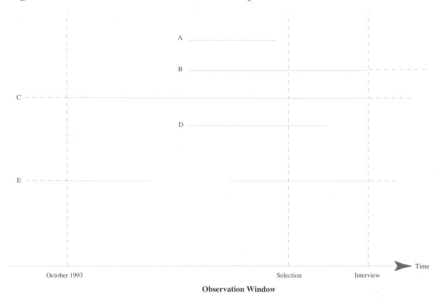

Part of the aim of this evaluation is to measure the length of time that people remain on benefit. The duration of unemployment up *until now* is a key measure available from the stock sample (the average incomplete duration), but this is a biased estimate of the likely duration on benefit for people starting a new claim. It is biased in two different directions. First, it may understate the duration of unemployment, since each spell is observed only up to the point of interview, not until the true end-point of unemployment. But, second, this estimate may be too long, for the simple reason that those with short spells of unemployment (like 'A' in Figure 8.6) tend to be excluded from the sample. In fact the chance than an individual will be selected into the stock sample is proportional to the length of his/her spell of unemployment.

Both biases are at work, simultaneously. Experience suggests that the latter effect is more important, so that stock samples *over-state* the likely duration of unemployment that will face new claims. It is worth adding that the average incomplete duration of unemployment (typically measured from samples of the unemployed) responds only slowly to changes in economic conditions. When a recession begins, larger inflows into unemployment result in an apparently shorter duration profile of the unemployed. During a recovery, inflows to unemployment fall, and hence the average duration of unemployment may rise (e.g. Corak, 1993).

It is these types of reason that justify taking a large cohort sample to be able to measure accurately the duration of unemployment through direct observation. Sampling for the flow, and estimates of duration from the flow sample, are quite a different matter. Figure 8.7 provides an illustration. Cases W to Z are included. All must have been receiving benefit for 14 days, or fewer, to be selected. They may have had no prior experience of unemployment (W, X, Z) or may have been unemployed either during the observation period or before it (Y).

Figure 8.7 Selection of the flow sample

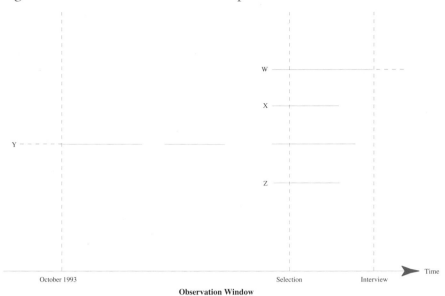

In time, the follow-up study will enable us to calculate durations of unemployment from the flow sample. As discussed above, there are important problems in calculating durations from the stock sample, (because of incomplete durations, and the fact that short-duration unemployed people are under-represented).

In this section we plan to look at 'spells' of activity and benefit status during the observation period. That is, any time during which someone is claiming benefit (Income Support or Unemployment Benefit), National Insurance credits, or neither. For now, we ignore time before the start of the observation window. To take an example, the person below (Figure 8.8) had two different 'spells' of activity during the observation window: the first when *not* claiming benefit, which was then followed by one where the respondent *was* on benefit. During the period from October 1993 to January 1994 she was not signing on. This spell is complete. During the spell from January 1994 until the interview she was on benefit: this is an incomplete spell of claiming benefit.

Figure 8.8 Changes of status during the observation period

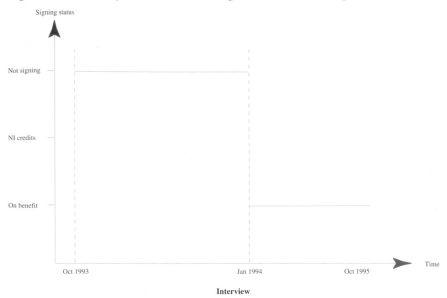

In total, the 4,876 respondents generated 15,242 different spells of signing or not signing. Allowing for sample weighting, 4,732 cases generated just over 12,000 different spells of signing, or not signing, during the time covered by the work and benefit history sheet.[2]

The first step in our analysis is to describe the average length of different types of spell. On average, those of the stock sample *still* unemployed had been unemployed for 58 weeks, compared with 20 weeks for those of the flow sample still unemployed. There is also data on completed spells – those in the past, but still taking place within the two-year observation window. Completed spells of signing on lasted an average of 28 weeks for the stock and 17 weeks for the flow. Since this ignores time unemployed prior to October 1993, it is likely to be an underestimate of the average length of unemployment, particularly for the stock sample.

There are a range of statistical models which attempt to combine data on both completed and incomplete spells, to arrive at an estimate of spell length that uses all available information. Such estimates are most useful for the flow sample. The estimated average length of unemployment was calculated to be 30 weeks for the flow. However this includes a small number of longer spells. The (very simple) model used here also suggests that **one-half of those *entering* claimant unemployment will have left within 21 weeks** (or just short of five months).

This type of analysis uses the retrospective information collected for the two years (or so) prior to interview. As emphasised, the selection of the stock sample acts to eliminate those with shorter durations of unemployment. The

---

2 In other words, the flow sample tended to move on and off benefit more frequently than the stock sample.

flow sample can be used to give a different picture of claim durations, but further analysis is limited by the very short time between selection and interviewing. The use of data from the second wave of fieldwork will allow much richer analysis to be conducted.

Table 8.4 gives the origins and destinations for 12,084 observed spells, some 4,732 of which were unfinished at the interview (that is, one per respondent). The sample can very roughly be said to contain one-third of spells which involve a move off benefit (31 per cent, circled), one-third being moves to signing-on (33 per cent, circled), and one-third of incomplete spells of unemployment (29 per cent, circled).

Table 8.4 Benefit origins and destinations during the observation window

					Total percentages
		Origin			
		Benefit	NI credits	Neither	Total
	Benefit	(29)*	1	(33)	63
Destination	NI credits	1	2*	3	6
	Neither	21	2	8*	(31)
	Total	51	5	44	100

* = unfinished spells

8.4 Conclusion   This chapter has looked at groups moving off benefit, and provided a preliminary analysis of durations on benefit. Movements off Income Support/Unemployment Benefit remain frequent. Retrospective and current evidence suggests that half of the newly unemployed will leave benefit within five months of signing on. This is a provisional estimate whose reliability will be much improved when the follow-up data have been analysed.

Men were less likely to have moved off benefit than women, and younger respondents found it easier to leave benefit than older ones. Those with a background in professional occupations were the most likely to have stopped signing, although status of itself was not a strong factor. Former managers tended to remain on benefit, in the short time observed, whilst those from certain lower-grade service occupations found it easier to move off benefit.

Most of those who left benefit had found paid work, with smaller numbers moving to any of quite a range of destinations. Men were more likely to have found full-time employment: although women also tended to move into full-time work, a sizeable proportion started part-time jobs. There was little use of in-work benefits and, if anything, most respondents did not encounter particular difficulties in moving into work. However a significant proportion of those unemployed for the longer times, felt they were worse off (or felt no improvement) when they moved into work. This was also true of respondents with young children. Those unemployed for less than six months, and those without children, tended to have more optimistic views of changes in living standards on leaving benefit.

9 MAIN CONCLUSIONS

On 7 October 1996, Jobseeker's Allowance was introduced nationwide, replacing Unemployment Benefit and Income Support for unemployed people. Writing in 1996, we may only speculate about the effects this will have. Some of the changes proposed are radical; others build on current practice. Some reforms are clear and straightforward to implement, such as the reduction to six months in contributory entitlement. The effectiveness of other changes, such as the Jobseeker's Agreement and Jobseeker's Directions, will depend in part on how they work 'on the ground'.

This report represents only the first few steps towards evaluating Jobseeker's Allowance, but is important in its own right as a survey of unemployment. It is based on perhaps the largest and most detailed national survey of unemployed claimants ever conducted in Britain, certainly since the important 1988 'Fowler' reform of social security, and the initiatives in government taken towards an Agency structure. In particular, this survey has collected uniquely detailed information about respondents' contacts with the Benefits Agency and the Employment Service, a range of information from claimants' partners, and high quality material about respondents' labour market history.

This report is based on the first of four national surveys of unemployed people being conducted as part of the evaluation: it is the first cohort, the first wave. Given this context, the aim has been to establish some of the baselines against which the impact of Jobseeker's Allowance can be assessed. In particular it has focused attention on:

- the labour market experiences of claimants before applying and receiving unemployment-related benefits

- their understanding of the contract between state and citizen implicit in the receipt of benefits

- the application process

- their job-search behaviour.

In addition results have been presented concerning the routes that people take off benefit. This will be a principal topic of the next report covering both interviews with the first cohort, ahead of the introduction of Jobseeker's Allowance. It is of course too early in the research to be reaching conclusions about the likely success of Jobseeker's Allowance. However, it is worth briefly drawing together the threads of the findings relating to experiences of unemployed claimants under the existing policy regime. And to draw attention to those aspects which are likely to be affected by, or to impinge on, the working of the new scheme.

9.1 Who are unemployed people?

The findings from the present survey are largely consistent with what is known about unemployed people from other sources. Certain findings warrant emphasis. First, it is widely appreciated that unemployed people tend to be drawn from low skilled occupations, have limited educational qualifications, and include comparatively large numbers of older and very young people.

While the survey confirms these findings, its structure enables distinctions to be made between the stock of unemployed claimants and the flow of new claimants. New claimants do share the above characteristics, but they are nevertheless less different from their contemporaries in work, than are the stock of unemployed. This points to a process in which the risk of unemployment is less concentrated on particular occupations than would be deduced from the stock alone, but that people with particular characteristics tend to get left behind on benefit as others find employment.

Moreover, the survey counsels against the assumption that unemployed people are socially homogenous. While people from technical or managerial occupations are less likely than manual workers to be become unemployed, they still account for more than one in five (21 per cent) of the stock. Moreover, the evidence suggests an increase in the number of unemployed with qualifications. This may indicate either that unemployment now affects groups that were previously unaffected, or the fact that the work-force is increasingly acquiring paper qualifications.

Another aspect of heterogeneity is the insecurity of employment for some claimants. Forty-six per cent of new claimants had never been unemployed before. The fact that fewer of the stock were in this position suggests that a good proportion of those experiencing their first spell of unemployment will rapidly find work. On the other hand, a disproportionate number of new claimants had already experienced unemployment. Indeed, on average new claimants had spent seven of the past 24 months out of work, a figure that understates the precarious labour market position of some groups since it is reduced by the records of those with no prior experience of unemployment.

Clearly, therefore, the majority of unemployed people in both the flow and stock have already been through the unemployment system and their living standards, attitudes and behaviour will, arguably, all be affected by this previous experience. Then again, eight per cent of the claimant unemployed, including those drawing National Insurance credits, had never worked. Some were young because they had just finished their education; others older and joining the labour market for the first time perhaps after a spell looking after a home or family.

Attention is sometimes focused on long-term unemployed people. In fact, a minority of the sample was unemployed for more than one year. However, as stressed in the preceding paragraph, others will have experienced repeated spells of unemployment, and some of the intervening spells in work may have been quite short. Moreover the survey showed that nine per cent reported being continuously unemployed for more than four years. Policy makers might expect this group to be smaller, if only because this group would have been expected to have undertaken some form of training – temporarily taking them off the claimant count. This may have been the reality for some, perhaps even all, of these respondents although it is probable that they still considered themselves to be unemployed during spells of training.

Finally, it is also worth drawing attention to the family circumstances of claimants. These varied widely, often at odds with the popular conception. Attention is often focused on families with children. This partly reflects public concern about the impact on children of being brought up in a work-less household, partly a concern that the financial demands of children are likely to increase the so-called reservation wage (a hypothesis this study supports), and partly the fact they receive higher levels of benefit. However, the survey reveals that only one in four claimants have dependent children and that the largest group were, in fact, single people, many living at home with their parents, though numbers of single people may have been raised during the summer sampling period.

9.2 Job-search and activities while unemployed

Eligibility for benefit requires claimants actively to look for work, and be available (and able) to take up paid work. As we discuss below, the nuances of the regulations had little salience for respondents. The vast majority were sufficiently keen on the prospect of the 'carrot' (employment) that they largely failed to notice the threat of the 'stick', the sanctions available if they failed to meet benefit rules.

The determination to work was reflected in the flexibility of jobs that people would accept, or consider accepting. Nine out of ten were prepared to work 40 or more hours a week. Three-quarters would have taken shift work or weekend work or would have taken one of a range of jobs (or indeed any job). More than half would have moved location to take a job, or at least considered doing so. If respondents were inflexible, their main inflexibility was to want full-time jobs as employees, although (even here) many were prepared to look at other options. The new rules concerning availability for work for at least 40 hours a week would, on this evidence, not cause a raised eyebrow for the vast majority of unemployed people.

In areas of high unemployment respondents were prepared to be more flexible in the range of work they were seeking. But the length of the claim appeared to make no difference to our index of flexibility. This cannot be interpreted as a simple cause and (no) effect. Perhaps most people do become more flexible over time, but those leaving unemployment were more flexible still. A single survey can't accurately pinpoint what happens to unemployed people over time.

However more than half the respondents admitted to temporary periods when disillusionment caused them to stop making applications, and almost as many felt luck had as much to do with getting a job as the amount of effort they put into looking for work. At this stage, we have little evidence to counter the latter view. There was a strong perception among respondents that it was the quality of applications that mattered, not the quantity. New claimants and women seemed more likely to obtain interviews and offers of employment, while people with paper qualifications seemed more successful at job interviews.

Only a very small proportion of current signers were not looking for work, or did not want to work. Some of their answers – particularly those relating to ill health – suggested they could at least consider alternative benefits. However, there was also evidence that a handful of claimants did not take the obligation to look for work seriously, and a number took (probably undeclared) paid work while signing. Whether these groups had desperately high levels of need, were showing blatant criminal dishonesty or ignorance of the system, is not something this study can readily address.

Unemployed people are permitted to undertake part-time work, some kinds of voluntary work and (with restriction) certain types of educational study whilst claiming benefit. It remains to be seen whether any of these activities assist the return to work, although some respondents believed they would, particularly those taking part in them. Almost one claimant in ten was doing some voluntary work, averaging six hours a week. At some stage about one in seven had taken a course of full-time study.

9.3 Rules, responsibilities and obligations

Jobseeker's Allowance is designed to emphasise and enforce the labour market obligations inherent in the receipt of unemployment-related benefits. Therefore considerable time was spent in the survey exploring claimants' understanding of obligations and a number of qualitative projects are currently underway to add further detail.

What has emerged to date has important ramifications. In summary, the vast majority of respondents accepted that it was their responsibility to look for work. Most were happy that claimants should be penalised if they did not fulfil their obligations. On the other hand, it was clear that respondents had only the broadest understanding of the rules associated with signing on for benefit, actively seeking or being available for work. Or, at least, they were only able to talk in generalities about them.

Moreover, there was also vagueness as to when disallowance or disqualification could come into play. Claimants tended to emphasise the role of sanctions as a response to benefit fraud (undeclared work), rather than to restrictions in job-search or availability. Indeed, many and, depending on the nature of the offence, sometimes most of those who had apparently been sanctioned were very surprised when this had happened.

It follows that many of the *principles* underlying Jobseeker's Allowance may prove to be acceptable to, and indeed supported by, unemployed claimants. However, the real challenge is how to convey the details relating to conditionality to people who had not grappled with them in the past and who may feel they have more important things to worry about.

The research points to some possibilities based on existing procedures and also some limitations. To begin with the latter, a large majority of respondents told interviewers that they followed their Back to Work Plan at least in part. However, it was evident that even those who adopted the plan generally followed it without any conviction that it would do any good. There were exceptions to this rule, most notably people who had had no prior experience of unemployment, but large numbers of respondents thought that the plan was no more than common sense and comparatively few admitted to changing their behaviour as a result of agreeing the plan. Jobseeker's Agreements are more detailed than Back to Work Plans. This may make them more difficult to follow in only broad terms. Unless claimants can be made to feel that their Agreement has greater intrinsic value than their previous Plans, being forced to follow the details is likely to become irksome and increase antagonism towards, and perhaps non-compliance with, the system.

On a more positive note, it is apparent that the active signing procedures may have some noticeable effects. Certainly, some respondents did mention taking action as a direct result of their last signing on interview, ranging from what might be considered very basic search activity, such as scanning the vacancy notice-boards in the Jobcentre, to applying for specific jobs and training courses. While it is not possible at this stage to assess whether the increased job-search activity that probably results from active signing bears fruit in the form of people moving into work, it seems unlikely to have the opposite effect. Moreover, it was clear that, at least in late Summer 1995, there was considerable scope for expanding the extent of active signing: in some offices the large majority of claimants reported some element of the active signing protocol being included on the last occasion, but in other offices active signing seemed to be more the exception than the rule.

It is not possible, at present, to say whether the positive impact of active signing can be sustained. Individuals may become bored and annoyed by constant checking and intervention, something that the next wave of research will investigate. Also, theoretically, it is possible that active signing will raise the overall level of job-search which, once the less difficult to fill vacancies have been filled, establishes a new equilibrium in which jobseekers are working harder at finding jobs but no more vacancies are being filled.

It is understood that new claims and Client Adviser interviews are also to be emphasised under Jobseeker's Allowance and again the survey reveals that there is scope for increasing activities in these areas. Fewer long-term unemployed respondents admitted to having had an interview with a Client Adviser than should have been expected. This suggests, either that some claimants are falling through the net or else that the interview was not particularly memorable. Half the people who could remember their interview had found it useful, a proportion which it might be hoped to increase, and 43 per cent took action as a result. The number of different actions that were suggested and the directions given to jobseekers was quite large, though not enormous, and in half of cases involved referral to what respondents described as Job Club – though they might have confused this with other Employment Service programmes like Job-search Seminars. Given that respondents span a range of experiences from the highly qualified to those with a history of mostly casual work, thought may need to be given to expanding the kind of opportunities that can be presented through client adviser interviews.

Finally, it is important to note that respondents who remembered their new claims interview and felt that it had helped them to decide the kinds of openings to pursue were also likely to recall that it contained pro-active elements such as advice on effective job-search and in-work benefits. It is possible that this is an example of respondents remembering what they wanted to remember: or perhaps what was most useful to remember. On the other hand, it may well indicate that what advisers put into the new claims interview is very important in determining clients' ongoing responses to it.

9.4 The follow-up data

This report has made comparisons between new cases, and existing cases; and used the duration of a claim to explain differences in outcomes and experiences. It has used the information about the two years prior to claiming, and the few weeks (or months) between sampling and interview. This ingenuity has enabled us to build up a picture of the process of unemployment in a number of ways. Those groups more common in the stock than the flow might be expected to have lower rates of leaving benefit. This has received confirmation corroboration by analysing those groups most likely to sign off between selection and interview. For example, women were able to sign off quicker than men; the young more rapidly than the old; professional people more quickly than the unskilled.

This ingenuity is no substitute for the information available from follow-up interviews. Analysis of a single survey is unable to distinguish clearly effects of being unemployed for longer from effects of different groups being more likely to become longer term unemployed.

The respondents described in this report were re-interviewed around six months later, when they were asked a similar range of questions. These new data will allow us to look at the average length of time people remain unemployed, and at how long they spend in various destinations – such as employment. Analysis will also show which groups of people, in which areas, and using which types of job-search methods, are the most (and least) likely to move into work or any other of the destinations off benefit. We look forward, with great interest, to the next steps in the analysis.

REFERENCES

Atkinson, A. and Micklewright, J. (1991) 'Unemployment Compensation and Labour Market Transitions: A Critical Review', *Journal of Economic Literature,* 29, 1679–1727.

Balls, E. and Gregg, P. (1993) *Work and Welfare: Tackling the Jobs Deficit* (Commission on Social Justice issue paper no. 3). London: Institute for Public Policy Research.

Boden. R. and Corden, A. (1994) *Measuring Low Incomes: Self-employment and Family Credit.* London: HMSO.

Bryson, A. and McKay, S. (Eds) (1994) *Is It Worth Working?: An Introduction to Some of the Issues.* London: Policy Studies Institute.

Corak, M. (1993) 'The Duration of Unemployment during Boom and Bust', *Canadian Economic Observer,* 4 September, 1–20.

Daniel, W. (1990) *The Unemployed Flow.* London: Policy Studies Institute.

Dawes, L. (1993) *Long-Term Unemployment and Labour Market Flexibility.* Centre for Labour Market Studies, University of Leicester.

Dobson, B., Beardsworth, A., Keil, T., and Walker, R. (1994) *Diet Choice and Poverty.* London: Family Policy Studies Centre.

Employment Department/Department of Social Security (1994) *Jobseeker's Allowance* (CM2687). London: HMSO.

Garman, A., Redmond, G. and Lonsdale, S. (1992) *Incomes In and Out Of Work: A Cohort Study of Newly Unemployed Men and Women* (Department of Social Security Research Report No. 7). London: HMSO.

Gaskin, K. and Davis Smith, J. (1995) *A New Civic Europe: A Study of the Extent and Role of Volunteering.* London: The Volunteer Centre, UK.

Gregg, P. (1993) 'Jobs and Justice: Why Job Creation Alone Will Not Solve Unemployment'. In Balls, E. and Gregg, P. (Eds) *Work and Welfare: Tackling The Jobs Deficit* (Commission on Social Justice issue paper no. 3). London: Institute for Public Policy Research.

Heady, P. and Smyth, M. (1989) *Living Standards during Unemployment.* London: HMSO.

Jones, T. (1993) *Britain's Ethnic Minorities*. London: Policy Studies Institute.

Kempson, E. (1996) *Living on a Low Income*. York: Joseph Rowntree Foundation.

McLaughlin, E., Millar, J. and Cooke, K. (1989) *Work and Welfare Benefits*. Aldershot: Avebury.

Mincer, J. (1974) *Schooling, Experience and Earnings*. New York: Columbia University Press.

Moylan, S., Millar, J. and Davies, R. (1984) *For Richer, For Poorer?: DHSS Cohort Study of Unemployed Men*. London: HMSO.

Nove, A. (1997) *Evaluation of JSA Cohort 1: Technical Report*. London Social and Community Planning Research.

Nove, A. with McKay, S. (1995) *Employment Service NCSS 1992–94: Extra Analysis of Disability Data* (Third Draft). London: Public Attitude Surveys Ltd.

Payne, J. and Payne, C. (1994) 'Recession, Restructuring and the Fate of the Unemployed', *Sociology*, 28, 1.

Poynter, R. and Martin, C. (1996) *Rights Guide to Non-means-tested Benefits*. London: Child Poverty Action Group.

Sainsbury, R., Hutton, S. and Ditch, J. (1996) *Changing Lives and the Role of Income Support* (Department of Social Security Research Report No. 45). London: HMSO.

Shaw, A., Walker, R., Ashworth, K., Jenkins, S. and Middleton, S. (1996) *Moving Off Income Support: Barriers and Bridges* (Department of Social Security Research Report No. 53). London: HMSO.

Shaw, A., Kellard, K. and Walker, R. (1996) *Barriers, Bridges and Behaviour: Learning from Income Support Recipients* (Department of Social Security In-house Report No. 18). London: Department of Social Security.

Stafford, B., Walker, R., Hull, L. and Horsley, E. (1996) *Customer Contact and Communication with the Benefits Agency: Literature Review* (Department of Social Security In-house Report No. 17). London: Department of Social Security.

Vincent, J., Walker, R., Dobson, B., Stafford, B., Barnes, M. and Bottomley, D. (1996) *Lone Parent Caseworker Pilots* (Draft Final Report)(Working Paper No. 263). Loughborough: Centre for Research in Social Policy.

Walker, R. (1995) *Benefits Agency Customers and the 1994 Review of the Benefits System.* (Department of Social Security In-house Report No. 7). London: Department of Social Security.

Walker, R., Shaw, A. and Kellard, K. (1994) *Trapped on Benefits? Barriers to Movement Off Income Support* (Working Paper No. 229). Loughborough: Centre for Research in Social Policy.

White, M. (1991) *Against Unemployment.* London: Policy Studies Institute.

White, M. and Lakey, J. (1992) The Restart Effect: Does Active Labour Market Policy Reduce Unemployment? London: Policy Studies Institute.

APPENDIX A

SAMPLING

APPENDIX A SAMPLING

Background   The sampling strategy was a crucial part of the evaluation. The population of interest was all unemployed claimants at the time of the survey. To ensure that the responses to the survey are representative of this population, the sampling strategy must be able to deal with the probable differences amongst claimant groups. Key considerations included:

- the intended sample size
- the stratification method
- the system used to provide the sample
- the sampling proportions.

The Appendix also discusses weighting. The weighting ensured that the obtained sample resembled the population as closely as possible and involved adjustments for the differential sampling proportions and different response rates within claimant subgroups. Further details of the sampling and weighting can be found in the technical report being produced by Social and Community Planning Research.

Sampling frame   The relevant population was all unemployed claimants at the time of the survey. There were several possible sources for this information. However, because systems are not equal in their size, currency or completeness, the final choice was unequivocal. The sampling frame used was the National Unemployment Benefit System (NUBS2).

A separate method was used to sample clerical (i.e. non-computerised) claims. These form an extremely small proportion of all claims (around two per cent) but a not-insubstantial proportion of new claims (ten per cent) and are typically more complex than most. It was decided that clerical cases represented such a small proportion of all claims that a special effort to extract them would have yielded little additional information. A sample of clerical claims was therefore taken for new claims only and these were selected from 25 offices to reduce administration inconvenience and costs.

Sample size   The research design involved the use of two two-wave cohorts: one sampled (and re-interviewed) before the introduction of Jobseeker's Allowance; the other following its implementation. A certain degree of attrition between waves is to be expected and the key to determining an adequate sample size was to work backwards from the desired number of responses at the second wave, taking into account estimated drop-outs.

It was decided that a second wave sample size of 3,000 provided the most appropriate balance between the better discriminatory power of a larger sample size and lower costs associated with a smaller sample. This would ensure a sufficient number of cases for analyses involving claimants belonging to most of the smaller sub groups. Assuming a drop-out or non-contact rate of 40 per cent between waves, this required a first-wave sample size of 5,000. To achieve this, 8,000 names and addresses were submitted to the fieldwork contractor (assuming a response rate of 60 per cent) and, assuming a 20 per cent opt-out rate, this required 10,000 claimants to be selected prior to opt-out.

Office stratification

Like many surveys of a geographically dispersed population, a multi-stage sampling methodology was adopted for reasons of cost and administrative efficiency. Claimants were grouped administratively at local Employment Service offices: these offices formed the primary sampling units of the sample. One hundred offices were chosen as it was felt that this number offered the most suitable compromise between the improved sampling error associated with a large number of offices and the simplified administration if a smaller number of offices was selected. It was calculated that 100 offices would ensure a measurement error in the region of nine per cent and that sampling from, say, 150 offices would not offer sufficient gain in precision to justify the extra costs and administration involved.

To ensure a representative sample of Employment Service offices, they were first grouped (using cluster analysis) by certain characteristics, such as unemployment rate in the travel-to-work area and register turnover, into similar clusters, defined within each region. The resultant 45 clusters then formed the strata from which the offices were selected.

Some offices were excluded from selection. These were geographically remote offices which would have been disproportionately expensive to survey and which typically contain such small fractions of the claimant population that omission will have minimal effect upon representativeness. The number of interviews to be achieved in each selected office was proportional to the size of the claimant register.

Claimant stratification

In the analysis, the behaviour and attitudes of new and existing claimants may be very different. Analytically, these two groups are likely to be equally important. To reflect this equality, it was felt that there should be equal proportions of new and existing claimants represented in the sample. Therefore, 5,000 each of new and existing claimants were selected to provide the 10,000 required for the pre-opt-out sample.

Claimants of different benefits may respond differently to the policy change, and it was therefore important that each claimant group as defined by benefit received (that is, those claiming: Income Support only; Unemployment Benefit only; both Income Support and Unemployment Benefit; and National Insurance Credits only) should have sufficient representation. Some of these claimants groups would be too small unless differential stratification was adopted. These groups were therefore over-sampled.

Using NUBS2 as the sampling frame had implications for categorisation of claimants by benefits received. It classifies claimants as one of: 'Income Support only'; 'Unemployment Benefit only'; 'Both Income Support and Unemployment Benefit'; and 'Neither Unemployment Benefit nor Income Support'. The last category contains those claiming National Insurance Credits, as well as those whose claims had not yet been assessed. More new claims will fall into this category, and it was therefore not possible to differentially sample by benefit type for new claimants; this was applied to existing claimants only.

Sampling proportions   As existing claimants were to be sampled according to their benefit group, appropriate sampling fractions had to be calculated. In order to achieve a sufficient number of interviews in each claimant group, it was felt that a sample of at least 700 in each group needed to be drawn. Therefore, to retain the overall sample size (5,000), some groups had to be under-sampled, others over-sampled. The targets for existing claimant interviews in each group were as shown in the table below.

Table A.1 Target interviews for existing claimants

Benefit group	Actual percentage of register in February 1995	Estimated sample size without under or over sampling	Sample target percentage	Sample target number of interviews	Degree of under or over sampling
Neither UB nor IS	9	445	16	800	1.8
UB only	13	665	22	1,100	1.7
IS only	72	3,575	48	2,400	0.7
UB and IS	6	315	14	700	2.2
Total	100	5,000	100	5,000	1.0

The next stage was to estimate the actual numbers that would be claiming in the selected offices at the time of sampling. The sampling fractions could then be calculated. Estimates were based on information for Great Britain in February 1995, making adjustments for the number of offices used and the time of the sampling (Summer 1995). The estimated figures are shown below, alongside the actual pre-opt-out sample size achieved.

Table A.2 Estimated numbers in each claimant group and pre-opt-out sample sizes

Benefit group	Estimated number of claimants	Percent of claimants	Pre-opt-out sample size	Pre-opt-out sample percents
New claimants	13,886	5	5,543	50
Existing claimants				
Neither UB nor IS	32,118	12	1,084	10
UB only	35,582	13	1,282	11
IS only	177,083	65	2,619	23
UB and IS	13,139	5	623	6
Total	271,808	100	11,151	100

The time of sampling may have had an important implication for the composition of the sample. Over the summer one would expect larger numbers of ex-students to claim benefits, and possibly a proportion of current students whom the rules should exclude. This is likely to affect the flow rather more than the stock, and Income Support cases rather than those on Unemployment Benefit.

Response rates

The issued sample was 7,699 claimants. When those who proved to be out of scope[1] were removed, this left 6,542 potential respondents. Interviews were obtained from 4,877 (75 per cent) of claimants. However, one interview turned out to have been conducted with the wrong person (the son having the same name as the father, both being unemployed) and was removed from the data, giving a final sample size of 4,876.

Data weighting

To ensure that the sample was representative of the population, weights were applied. A two-stage weighting procedure was adopted to account for both the differential sampling proportions explained in the preceding sections, and differential response rates by personal characteristics.

The first stage of weights were derived from:

(Proportion in claimant group in population x total pre-opt-out sample size) Pre-opt-out sample size in each claimant group

This ensured that those groups over-sampled are weighted down, and those under-sampled are weighted up, as shown in Table A.3.

---

1 For reasons such as: follow-up addresses not being known; moved out of area; late opt-out, etc.

Table A.3 First-stage weights

Benefit group	Proportion in population	Pre-opt-out sample	First-stage weight
New claimants	.05	5,543	.10
Existing claimants			
Neither UB nor IS	.12	1,084	1.22
UB only	.13	1,282	1.13
IS only	.65	2,619	2.77
UB & IS	.05	623	.86
Total	1.0	11,151	

Applying these weights gave a sample representative of all claimants. This ensured, for instance, that just five per cent of new claimants were incorporated into this sample. These weights were not applied for analyses on new claimants only.

A second stage of weighting was incorporated to allow for the fact that some groups had different response rates. To do this, the characteristics of non-respondents as well as respondents were needed and so the characteristics incorporated into this analysis were restricted to those available from NUBS2. These were: age; gender; duration of claim; and benefit group. A CHAID (Chi-Square Automatic Interaction Detector) segmentation model was used to identify groups with significantly different response rates. The variables which produced significant differences were: age; benefit received (for those in the younger age groups only); and duration of claim (within the older age groups only). According to these response rates, a second set of weights were calculated.

For all claimants, the resulting weight was therefore the product of the two sets of weights described. For 'new claimants only' analyses, just this second set of weights were applied.

OTHER RESEARCH REPORTS AVAILABLE:

No.	Title	ISBN	Price
1.	Thirty Families: Their living standards in unemployment	0 11 761683 4	£6.65
2.	Disability, Household Income and Expenditure	0 11 761755 5	£5.65
3.	Housing Benefit Reviews	0 11 761821 7	£16.50
4.	Social Security and Community Care: The case of the Invalid Care Allowance	0 11 761820 9	£9.70
5.	The Attendance Allowance Medical Examination: Monitoring consumer views	0 11 761819 5	£5.50
6.	Lone Parent Families in the UK	0 11 761868 3	£12.75
7.	Incomes In and Out of Work	0 11 761910 8	£17.20
8.	Working the Social Fund	0 11 761952 3	£9.00
9.	Evaluating the Social Fund	0 11 761953 1	£22.00
10.	Benefits Agency National Customer Survey 1991	0 11 761956 6	£16.00
11.	Customer Perceptions of Resettlement Units	0 11 761976 6	£13.75
12.	Survey of Admissions to London Resettlement Units	0 11 761977 9	£8.00
13.	Researching the Disability Working Allowance Self Assessment Form	0 11 761834 9	£7.25
14.	Child Support Unit National Client Survey 1992	0 11 762060 2	£30.00
15.	Preparing for Council Tax Benefit	0 11 762061 0	£5.65
16.	Contributions Agency Customer Satisfaction Survey 1992	0 11 762064 5	£18.00
17.	Employers' Choice of Pension Schemes: Report of a qualitative study	0 11 762073 4	£5.00
18.	GPs and IVB: A qualitative study of the role of GPs in the award of Invalidity Benefit	0 11 762077 7	£12.00
19.	Invalidity Benefit: A survey of recipients	0 11 762087 4	£10.75

43.	Paying for Rented Housing	0 11 762370 9	£19.00
44.	Resettlement Agency Customer Satisfaction Survey 1994	0 11 762371 7	£16.00
45.	Changing Lives and the Role of Income Support	0 11 762405 5	£20.00
46.	Social Assistance in OECD Countries: Synthesis report	0 11 762407 1	£22.00
47.	Social Assistance in OECD Countries: Country report	0 11 762408 X	£47.00
48.	Leaving Family Credit	0 11 762411 X	£18.00
49.	Women and Pensions	0 11 762422 5	£35.00
50.	Pensions and Divorce	0 11 762423 5	£25.00
51.	Child Support Agency Client Satisfaction Survey 1995	0 11 762424 1	£22.00
52.	Take Up of Second Adult Rebate	0 11 762390 3	£17.00
53.	Moving off Income Support	0 11 762394 6	£26.00
54.	Disability, Benefits and Employment	0 11 762398 9	£30.00
55.	Housing Benefit and Service Charges	0 11 762399 7	£25.00
56.	Confidentiality: The public view	0 11 762434 9	£25.00
57.	Helping Disabled Workers	0 11 762434 3	£25.00
	Social Security Research Yearbook 1990–91	0 11 761747 4	£8.00
	Social Security Research Yearbook 1991–92	0 11 761883 0	£12.00
	Social Security Research Yearbook 1992–93	0 11 762150 1	£13.75
	Social Security Research Yearbook 1993–94	0 11 762302 4	£16.50
	Social Security Research Yearbook 1994–95	0 11 762362 8	£20.00
	Social Security Research Yearbook 1995–96	0 11 762446 2	£23.00
59.	Delivering Social Security: A cross-national study	0 11 762447 0	£35.00
60.	A Comparative Study of Housing Allowances	0 11 762448 9	£26.00
61.	Lone Parents, Work and Benefits	0 11 762450 0	£25.00

Further information regarding the content of the above may be obtained from:

Department of Social Security
Attn. Keith Watson
Social Research Branch
Analytical Services Division 5
10th Floor, Adelphi
1–11 John Adam Street
London WC2N 6HT
Telephone: 0171 962 8557

Printed in the United Kingdom for The Stationery Office.
Dd.303588, 3/97, C12, 3397/5, 5673, 365015.